SO-EBT-544

UNIONS
AND THE PUBLIC
INTEREST

UNIONS
AND THE PUBLIC
INTEREST

Collective bargaining
in the government sector

Sandra Christensen

THE FRASER INSTITUTE
1980

The Fraser Institute is pleased to acknowledge financial support from the Max Bell Foundation for the project series, Unions and the Public Interest.

Canadian Cataloguing in Publication Data

Christensen, Sandra.

Unions and the public interest

(Labour market series; no. 2)
Bibliography: p.
ISBN 0-88975-022-X

1. Trade unions — Government employees —
Canada. 2. Collective bargaining — Government
employees — Canada. I. Fraser Institute,
Vancouver, B.C. II. Title. III. Series.
HD8013.C23C57   331.88'1135471   C80-091216-0

Contents

v

Preface & Summary

[It is] the business of a union to be anti-social; the members would have a just grievance if their officials and committees ceased to put sectional interests first.

Barbara Wootton
Labour Party Peer in the
U.K. House of Lords

This remarkably courageous statement by a leading left-wing intellectual and social activist presents a challenge to conventional thinking about unions and their impact on the public interest. The general public has for years been exposed to the vision of the long-suffering union struggling against enormous odds to improve the lot of all workers. In the context of this vision, many Canadians, whether union members or not, have implicitly sympathized with the aims of the union and, as electors, have ratified their activities. Legislation in Canada and the United States, in general, supports the activities of unions and exempts them from the scrutiny that is accorded other groups which might combine against the public interest.

The image conjured up by Lady Barbara Wootton is entirely different. It depicts the union as a self-serving, "sectional" force whose object is to improve the lot of its members at the expense of the general public—including other union members. This view of unions as an essentially self-serving, anti-social element in our midst would, if it were widespread, provoke a very different response on the part of the general public. Unions, like corporations and other institutions of self-interest, would be surveyed more skeptically by all in the hope that vigilance would protect the public interest.

The Fraser Institute has initiated a series of studies under the general heading, "Unions and the Public Interest," to investigate the behaviour of unions—how they have behaved and how they are likely to behave in the future. This study, by Professor Sandra Christensen 'of Simon Fraser University, is the first study in the series and concerns itself with the behaviour of unions in the government sector.

Importance of public sector unions

The importance of union activity in this sector to the well-being of our country cannot be over-estimated. One out of five people in the active work force is employed in the governmental sector and some nine-tenths of them are unionized. As a direct consequence, nearly half of total union membership in Canada is employed by governments and public administration is the most heavily unionized of all the major sectors in our economy.

The behaviour of government or quasi-government employee unions, therefore, has a potentially sizeable effect on wages in the economy. Moreover, in the light of the observation that unions are essentially self-serving institutions, the ability of public sector unions to withdraw their services and prevent others from replacing them represents an on-going threat to the public interest. While this is generally true, it is particularly true of those services which are provided by government, in preference to the private sector, because of their allegedly "essential" nature. Often as not, government is a monopoly supplier of these services.

The strike threat system

As Professor Christensen documents, the spread of unionization of government employees was accompanied by a marked increase in the incidence of strikes in the public sector. While in the first half of the 1960s man-days lost per employee in the public sector were only 10 per cent of man-days lost per employee in the private sector, by the first half of the 1970s this ratio had grown to 35 per cent. Thus, while strike activity is still modest by comparison with the private sector, there has been a dramatic increase in its incidence in the public sector. Moreover, as Christensen points out, since there are many reasons to expect a lower strike rate amongst public employees (outright prohibition in the case of police and firemen and other public employees in five out of 10 provinces, for example) the incidence rate, on a comparable basis, may be higher than it appears.

A significant aspect of public sector strike activity found by Christensen is that the strikes in the public sector are much shorter, on average, than private sector strikes. The implication is that "the political cost of strikes in the public sector (in terms of public resentment at the inconvenience) are so great that the public employer quickly accedes to union demands or induces the government to intercede with ad hoc legislation." Dr. Christensen's examination of the performance of public sector wages as compared with private sector wages, suggests that government, as employer, has been more inclined to give in to union demands.

Public versus private wages

"The growth of public sector earnings relative to those in the private sector has occurred in all parts of the public sector, with the most rapid gains being made by teachers and federal government employees... most public sector employees have surpassed wage parity with the private sector."

Although the extent to which public earnings exceed private earnings is as high as 30 per cent in the case of teachers and professors, it averages out at about nine per cent. This is likely to be an underestimate of the differential since it takes no account of the shorter average work week and longer vacation entitlement in the public sector. Moreover, the presumed stability of government employment and the more generous pension provisions serve to make public employment even more attractive.

"The implication of this evidence is that the government is not just a 'good' employer; it has become one of the 'best' employers in the economy. While the logic of the prevailing wage principle implies that the public sector should take its lead from private sector compensation packages, Canada in recent years has seen the reversal of this principle, so that now private sector employees are pointing to gains made in the public sector to justify their bargaining demands. Further, the pay advantage now enjoyed by public sector employees arose simultaneously with the rise of public sector unionism. This, in itself, does not prove that current legislation is too permissive regarding union activity in the private sector, but it does offer considerable support to that view."

Public sector labour laws most liberal in world?

Although there are still some significant differences between labour policy for the private and public sectors, Canada's public employees have virtually all of the unionization rights given to the private sector. In sweeping changes to federal and provincial legislation during the mid-1960s, wages were made subject to collective bargaining everywhere and the strike weapon was made legally available to many public sector workers.

By comparison with the United States and the United Kingdom, after whose labour legislation Canada's was modelled, these developments represented quite a radical departure. In the United States, federal and most state government employees are prohibited from striking and are

xii

not permitted to bargain over wages. Canadian policy also contrasts sharply with labour legislation in Britain where wages in the public sector are not normally determined by bargaining but rather by strict adherence to private sector comparability guidelines.

Since provinces set their own laws relating to the conduct of public sector unions, it is not surprising to find quite a variance in the codes — particularly the provisions relating to the right to strike. In the latter regard, the legislation in the provinces ranges from permissive to prohibitive with British Columbia and Saskatchewan on the permissive end and Alberta, Ontario, and P.E.I. on the prohibitive end. Federal labour relations policy is similar to that in the more permissive of the provinces. In both federal and provincial labour relations there are some issues which are not negotiable. For the most part, these relate to promotion and benefits provided under separate statutes.

Differences between private and public sector

To a considerable extent, the treatment of public sector unions in current labour legislation reflects the belief that employees in the public sector should be treated in the same way as employees in the private sector.

Nevertheless, Professor Christensen maintains that there are important differences between the public sector and private sector that should make us wary about the unfettered transfer of union rights from the private sector into the public sector. In the first place, the normal disciplines of the marketplace are not exerted on the wages the public sector union can successfully demand. Higher wage costs are not immediately reflected in higher prices for the government service involved. As a consequence, the union can make its demands with the knowledge that there will be no immediate economic consequence. In many instances, the economic effects of a wage increase can be lateralized and forced on some other aspect of public service. Higher wages for teachers, for example, may well lead to less expenditure on sports equipment or grounds maintenance rather than fewer jobs for teachers. Even restrictions on teacher employment tend to be exercised by restricting hiring rather than laying off current employees.

The private sector employer is primarily interested in maintaining an adequate rate of return on the capital employed by the firm. As a consequence, he will, in most instances, resist wage increases that exceed productivity gains. Failure to do so, especially in export-related industries where prices are internationally determined, would lead to a direct loss for the employer and the threat that profits, and hence return on invested capital, will fall below a level compatible with the firm's survival.

The vote motive versus the profit motive

In the public sector, the employer is effectively a group of politicians attempting to maximize its voter appeal. While one aspect of that appeal is the cost of government services and the extent, therefore, to which the costs of government are kept under control, a much more visible and important factor is the supply of government services. An increase in taxes occasioned by giving in to a union's demands is spread across all taxpayers and is of minimal significance to each individual. An interruption of service, like a postal strike or teachers' strike, has very sizeable, direct effects on taxpayers. Politicians faced with the prospect of higher wages or interrupted service will usually find the former to be more attractive. According to Christensen, the empirical analysis is consistent with this view and public sector wages appear, in contrast to private sector wages, to be completely insensitive to labour market conditions.

"In the private sector the strike is an economic weapon; but in the public sector it is a political weapon. The public employer suffers no financial loss during a work stoppage. Tax revenues are collected, whether or not there are disruptions in service. But, partly for that reason, the

political costs to the public em
are often substantial. By capi
costs, employee unions may inc
public budget... they may cha
some public services are provide(
a host of other issues, all of whic
should be decided jointly by the
not to say that the employees are
affected; of course they are. But
that public, and the full tr_____ or collective
bargaining to the public sector may result in such disproportionate power for employee groups that the interests
of the rest of the public are unprotected.''

With this assessment in hand, Professor Christensen
discusses a variety of public policy alternatives that might
"balance the desire of public employees to exercise some
control over their working conditions against the broader
public interest.''

PUBLIC POLICY PROPOSALS
On wage determination
Public sector wage determination should be guided by the
"prevailing wage principle.''

"The prevailing wage principle is founded on the equity
and efficiency of maintaining comparability between
public and private sector compensation levels. There is
apparently widespread public acceptance of its justice.
When public employees may bargain and strike over compensation, the principle of comparability with the private
sector is effectively replaced by the principle of more pay
to those with more power.''

In Professor Christensen's view, the fundamental problem is
that public employees are permitted to bargain over
compensation levels at all.

...ld fashion a new public sector labour policy, we
...advocate a system in which overall compensation
...s were not negotiable. The overall level of compen-
...ation for each job type would be determined in each
jurisdiction by an independent and continuing wage
board, whose decisions would be based on strict private
sector comparability guidelines.''

The members of the Wage Board would be selected on a
broad basis and enjoy complete independence, similar to
Supreme Court Justices, by virtue of a lengthy appointment
term. The Board would welcome submissions from employers
and employees and would monitor compensation levels,
employee turnover, and other aspects of public employment to
ensure that comparability was, in fact, obtained. Since the
research function for such boards already exists in the form of
the Pay Research Bureau and personnel are already employed
as arbitrators, there need be no increase in the number of
bureaucrats. A wages board system would simply involve
different sorts of people employed in a more effective way.

On the right to strike

"Since the level of compensation would not be subject
to collective bargaining, strikes to win increased compensation would be prohibited.''

In calling for a prohibition of the strike in the public sector,
Professor Christensen draws a sharp distinction between
compensation and working conditions. While issues related to
compensation should not be bargainable, non-compensation
issues should be and employees should be permitted to
withdraw their labour in support of their bargaining position.
Thus, while the strike weapon could not be used to "hold
the public up for ransom" for higher wages, it could be used to
"right a wrong" perceived by employees. Since wages would
be determined by the independent Wage Board, a strike on a

non-compensation issue could not be used in a lateral way to extract higher wages from the public employer. (Though, of course, the Wage Board would come under considerable indirect political pressure.)

On the right to retaliate

The main argument cited by opponents of public sector strikes is that public services, by their very nature, ought not to be interrupted by work stoppages. And, certain of the services supplied by the public sector — as well as the private sector — ought not to be interruptable if that would pose a serious threat to public health or security. For the most part, however, it is public inconvenience rather than public safety that is at stake and, in this light, Professor Christensen proposes several actions that would strengthen the hand of public employers and reduce the vulnerability of the services they provide.

First, public employers should engage in a wide-ranging program of *contingency planning.* This would include alternative ways of delivering a service, designation of employee positions as "essential", and limiting union security clauses to the Rand formula. The latter provision would enable those workers who did not support a strike to report for work without fear of expulsion from the union and, hence, loss of their job.

Second, public employers must be given the flexibility to respond to successful union demands by making *adjustments in their work force.* If public employees become too expensive, public employers must have the right to automate functions or contract them out to companies in the private sector. Layoffs — not simply attrition — must become a feasible form of public sector employment adjustment. Perhaps most importantly, public sector employers must be given the right to employ the lockout against employees striking on a rotating basis. (Currently this is permitted only in British Columbia.) In conjunction with the lockout, public employers should have the right to hire replacements for striking employees and lay off non-striking employees idled by the strike.

Third, the public sector employers ought to give more public exposure to salary levels and rates of advancement in the public service. In particular, these should be highlighted at times when negotiations are in process. Knowledge of public sector compensation levels may make the general public more tolerant of interruptions in service and less anxious to force a settlement. Also, tax revenues not required to pay striking public employees should be returned to taxpayers by means of tax reductions.

Fourth, in the event of illegal work stoppages, amnesty should not be available through the bargaining process. That is, it should not be possible for union members to seek amnesty for past actions as part of an emerging collective agreement.

Practical issues

In making her proposals, Professor Christensen is careful to note the practical difficulties involved. She draws particular attention to the difficulties a Wage Board would have in defining wage comparability given the differences between public and private sector employment. On the other hand, she is quite sanguine that after an initial period of adjustment, market forces (in the form of resignations or applications for public employment) can be relied upon to provide the Wage Board with enough information to "fine tune" wages and benefit structures.

The most serious roadblock foreseen by Christensen is the lack of political courage to withdraw bargaining privileges universally available to public sector employees. In recognizing this problem, she notes an aspect of the proposed changes that could ease the political difficulties posed. That is, the fact that a Wage Board would be in the interest of public sector employees in the long term. Historical experience in Canada suggests that governments have often used public sector wages as a scapegoat during times of restraint. The most recent evidence on this score is provided by the relative success governments achieved in controlling public sector wages during the 1975-1978 wage and price control program. An independent Wage Board would not only protect the taxpayer from excessive gains by public employees, it would also protect public employees from inappropriate measures taken against them by government during periods of public sector belt-tightening. Thus, it may be in the interest of public employees to accept a curtailment of their bargaining rights even though that does not appear, superficially, to be desirable.

The Fraser Institute has been pleased to initiate this series of studies on unions and the public interest and gratefully acknowledges the financial support of the Max Bell Foundation. Moreover, the Institute welcomes the opportunity to publish Professor Christensen's work. However, because the author's conclusions were arrived at independently, the views expressed may not conform singly or collectively with those of the Institute's members or funding agencies.

August 1980   Michael Walker

About the Author

Sandra Christensen, an assistant Professor of Economics at Simon Fraser University, Burnaby, British Columbia, was born in Chattanooga, Tennessee, in 1944 and took her undergraduate degree at Florida State University. From there, she went to the University of Wisconsin-Madison for graduate work in Economics, receiving her Ph.D. in Economics in 1972.

Professor Christensen was a teaching assistant at the University of Wisconsin-Madison (1968/69), an Assistant Professor at the University of Maryland-College Park (1971-73), and in 1974 moved to Simon Fraser University. She has also served as a Research Associate, Project on the Economics of Discrimination, at the University of Maryland; a Consultant to the Equal Employment Opportunity Commission and an Economist with the Office of the Secretary (Planning and Evaluation) in the Department of Health, Education, and Welfare, both in Washington, D.C.

Articles by Professor Christensen have appeared in academic journals in Canada and the United States. She was also a participant in an earlier Fraser Institute book in this Labour Market Series, *Unemployment Insurance: Global Evidence of its Effects on Unemployment.*

Introduction

Just prior to the imposition of wage and price controls in 1975, Canada had attained the unenviable distinction of having one of the worst records in terms of man-days lost due to work stoppages of any of the Western industrialized economies. Further, the magnitude of the pay increases that unionized employees were demanding (and sometimes getting) was alarming, since pay increases so much in excess of the average increase in productivity were likely to lead to accelerating inflation, still higher unemployment, or both, depending on the money supply and exchange rate responses permitted by the central bank. The public was inclined to blame unionized labour for a good part of Canada's economic problems, and the public mood seemed to favour the imposition of greater constraints on union activities.

It is the purpose of this study to examine the activities of organized labour in one sector of our economy—the public sector—in order to determine whether further constraints on public sector union activity are justified by the public interest. The implications of our analysis suggest that there are fundamental objections to the current trend toward the blanket extension to public sector unions of privileges enjoyed by unions in the private sector.

After describing the current state of union activity in the

public sector and the legal environment in which public sector unions operate at present, we point out important differences between public and private sector bargaining relationships which we think justify a corresponding difference in labour relations policy between the two sectors. Our recommendations for public sector labour relations policy are contained in the concluding sections.

CHAPTER ONE
Union Activity in the Public Sector

HIGH MEMBERSHIP LEVELS

Over the decade of the 1960s, Canada has experienced major changes in the characteristics of her labour force. The labour force has become substantially younger, better educated, and more concentrated in white-collar, service occupations than previously. However, the change of most interest for our purposes is the large increase in unionization which has occurred in the public sector, largely in response to more permissive legislation in the provincial and federal jurisdictions.[1]

The figures in Table 1 show that the proportion of employees in public administration at all levels (local, provincial, and federal) who are union members has increased from 23 per cent in 1962 to almost 70 per cent in the late 1970s. Most of this growth in public sector union membership represents a transformation of existing public employee associations into formally certified unions, rather than the organization of new groups of workers. Nevertheless, the transformation of employee associations into unions has significant implications for the state of labour relations in Canada. It means that a greater proportion of the public sector labour force is now organized for formal collective bargaining, often including the strike as a legitimate bargaining tactic. Indeed, as a comparison across the industrial groups presented in Table 1 shows, public administration is now the most heavily unionized of all the major industrial sectors in our economy.

NEAR UNIVERSAL COVERAGE

Another indication of the extent of union influence in the public sector is given by the proportion of employees covered by a collective agreement, some of whom will not be union members.[2] Among public service office employees at the local, provincial, and federal levels, 89 per cent were covered by collective agreement in 1977; among public service non-office employees, 94 per cent were covered by collective agreement. These figures are presented in Table 2, in which coverage figures for other major industries are also given for comparison. As Table 2 indicates, the proportion of employees covered by collective agreement is substantially higher in public administration than in any of the other major industrial sectors reported. In fact, the coverage of union-negotiated settlements is nearly complete among civil servants at the three levels of public administration. The figures given here do not include those working in hospitals and schools, or in other government sectors (most notably, the Post Office) that are not part of public administration as defined by Statistics Canada; nor do they include employees of Crown corporations. However, the employees in these sectors, too, have been unionized rapidly since the 1960s. If public service employment is broadly defined to include not only public administration, but also postal workers, teachers, hospital employees, and employees of Crown corporations, then public service employees represent close to half the total union membership in Canada.[3]

IMPACT ON THE ECONOMY

The extent of unionization in the public sector is great. When that fact is considered in conjunction with the impor-

4

tance of the government (at all three levels) as employer, the potential impact of union activity in the public sector on the economy as a whole is considerable. If only civil servants and employees of Crown corporations are counted, about one out of every seven Canadian employees worked for one of Canada's governments. If hospital employees, teachers, and the armed forces are counted in as well, then close to one in five Canadian employees are in the public sector.[4] This means that wage gains made in the public sector are going to have a sizeable effect on average earnings levels in Canada, even before any consideration is made of the demonstration effect that public sector gains may have on the private sector. Further, because of the widespread activity of government today, work stoppages in the public sector are bound greatly to inconvenience the public, grown accustomed to existing services, even if they are not an immediate threat to health or safety. In the following sections, we shall examine data on work stoppages and compensation in order to assess the impact of unionization in the public sector.

GROWING INCIDENCE OF LABOUR UNREST

Increased strike activity by public employees is one of the considerations which has led to current misgivings about labour relations law as it now applies to the public sector. The data in Table 3.a are work stoppage figures for public employees in education, health, welfare, and public administration at all three levels of government. The figures presented cover the period during which public sector unionization was growing rapidly, up until the introduction of wage and price controls in 1975. Annual figures are averaged over five-year intervals in order to eliminate meaningless annual variations in work stoppage levels which arise only because of annual variations in the number of expiring contracts.

The percentage data show the incidence of work stoppages in the public sector relative to work stoppages for the whole economy. Since a significant portion of public sector labour

5

unrest occurs in the Post Office, we would like to be able to include postal employees in the public-sector counts in Table 3. The data do not permit identification of postal workers alone, but we can add the whole of the communications industrial grouping to the public sector counts to get upper-bound estimates of public sector labour unrest relative to the whole economy. (The communications sector includes radio, television, and telegraph workers, in addition to postal employees.) With this adjustment, we obtain the figures presented in Table 3.b. These figures indicate that work stoppages in the public sector are a growing component of labour unrest in our economy, whether measured in terms of number of stoppages, number of workers involved, or man-days lost.

GROWTH IN LABOUR UNREST MORE RAPID THAN EMPLOYMENT OR UNIONIZATION

The figures in Table 3 should be put in perspective, though, by comparing them to the proportion of the total labour force which is employed in the public sector. In Table 4.a, we have compiled figures on work stoppages per employee in the public sector, and reported those as a percentage of work stoppages per employee in the whole economy. From these, it is clear that the growth in employment in the public sector is not sufficient to explain the growth in public sector labour unrest relative to the rest of the economy. In the 1960-64 period, man-days lost per employee due to work stoppages in the public sector were only five per cent of man-days lost per employee in the whole economy; by the 1970-74 period, this had risen to 45 per cent. Hence, the incidence of labour unrest in the public sector has risen substantially, even after standardizing for the relative growth in employment in that sector.

Since it is difficult for non-unionized employees to organize a work stoppage, some increase in labour unrest in the public sector is to be expected, given the very rapid rise in unionization over the period examined. However, in Table 4.b, we present the same work stoppage figures per *unionized* employee.

6

The same general conclusion results. The incidence of labour unrest in the public sector has risen substantially, even after standardizing for the relative growth in unionized employment in that sector.[5]

It is this substantial increase in the incidence of labour unrest in the public sector which has helped to generate current public dissatisfaction with public sector labour relations policy. However, many viewing the figures in Table 4 may be surprised to see that, despite its substantial increase, public sector labour unrest remains disproportionately low. If work stoppages per employee were as prevalent in the public sector as they are in the private sector, each of the ratios in Table 4 would be close to 100. Instead, we find that the number of work stoppages and the number of man-days lost per employee in the public sector were less than half that experienced in the whole economy during the 1970-74 period.

There are three different considerations which may all be important in accounting for the differential incidence of labour unrest:

1) As is explained later, in Chapter V, the public employer typically has less incentive than the private sector employer to resist the demands of his employees, and, therefore, occasions in which a strike is necessary to back demands occur less frequently than in the private sector;

2) a substantial proportion of unionized employees in the public sector is legally prohibited from striking. These include most police and firefighters, as well as employees in provincial public administration in five out of the 10 provinces. By contrast, there are very few limitations on the right to strike for employees in the private sector; and

3) the public sector has a higher proportion of white-collar and professional employees in its work force than is typical of the private sector. Professional employees seem, in general, to be less supportive of the strike as a bargaining tactic. It would be informative to present the figures contained in Table 4 separately for office and non-office employees, but this break-down is not available from published work stoppage data.

7

DURATION OF WORK STOPPAGES

The large discrepancy between number of workers involved in public sector strikes and the number of man-days lost, relative to the corresponding figures for the economy as a whole, indicates that the duration of strikes in the public sector is considerably shorter, on average, than in the private sector. This is consistent with one of the arguments made by those who favour a return to more restrictive labour legislation for the public sector; i.e., that the political costs of strikes in the public sector (in terms of public resentment at the inconvenience) are so great that the public employer quickly accedes to union demands, or induces the government to intercede with *ad hoc* legislation. This argument would maintain that though the number of work stoppages may still be relatively small in the public sector, when they do occur they involve so many workers and have such significant effects on the general public—a third party not directly involved in the dispute—that they should not be permitted at all. The sentiment sometimes expressed is that if a service is important enough to be provided publicly, then it is important enough to be provided without interruption. Consequently, if we are going to permit the strike to any given group of public employees, the conclusion that might be drawn is that the service they provide is not important enough to justify public provision and should be returned to the private sector.

CHAPTER TWO

Public vs. Private Gains in Compensation

Increased strike activity is only one of the factors causing misgivings about public sector labour policies. A second basis for current misgivings about labour relations law as it applies to the public sector is the fear that current legislation gives employee unions too much power to extract wage and other gains at the expense of the public employer and the tax-paying public.

A. THE CRITERION OF COMPARABILITY

There appears to be widespread acceptance of the "prevailing wage" principle, that wage scales in the public sector should be comparable to those paid by a "good" employer in the private sector, that the public sector should neither lead nor lag the private sector in the total package of pay and fringes. To implement this principle in the federal sector, the Pay Research Bureau has, since 1957, conducted regular surveys of both public and private sector pay scales and fringe benefits. This information is made available to employer and employee negotiators, and is supposed to serve as a guide to the reasonable resolution of disputes over compensation.

The principle of the prevailing wage is sensible in terms of both equity and efficiency.

"The output of government does not pass through the marketplace where its relative worth can be assessed by customers. In the absence of a product market discipline imposed on pay practices...what could be more fair than to pay government employees what their private industry counterparts are getting? To attract employees of at least average quality to the government, the pay offered must be comparable to that available in the private sector. For the government to pay more than the private sector, however, would be unnecessary and would waste government revenues."[6]

B. PROBLEMS IN IMPLEMENTING THE COMPARABILITY CRITERION

Despite the logic and rhetorical acceptance of the prevailing wage principle by both public sector unions and management, its implementation has not been without problems. There are three problems that are particularly troublesome.

1) There is a wide range of wages paid for most private sector jobs. Hence, though both sides may espouse the prevailing wage principle, there is ample room for disagreement about how to define the prevailing wage. The Treasury Board, which serves as public employer in much of the federal sector, advocates the average wage, by occupation, obtained from a sample survey of all private sector employers (a 100 per cent universe). Union representatives, however, oppose this definition and favour instead the average wage, by occupation, obtained from a sample survey of only the larger private sector employers (a 75 per cent, or even a 50 per cent universe). The more selective universe would result in a larger measure of the prevailing wage, since large enterprises typically pay higher wages than small enterprises.[7]

2) As often practiced, the prevailing wage principle is viewed narrowly as applying to wage compensation alone, without regard to fringes and working conditions. But,

"any reasonably sophisticated view of the labour market recognizes that the wage is merely the most variable part of employment compensation, the part that firms most easily adjust to offset other aspects of compensation (fringe benefits, working conditions, location, etc.) that are discernibly advantageous or disadvantageous. A private firm can experiment with its wage rates, relative to those of other firms, in order to discover the rates that, along with other characteristics of the firm, will attract an adequate work force. In contrast, government employers required to pay prevailing wages almost always interpret that requirement as precluding any attempt to take into account the attractiveness of non-wage aspects of government employment.''[8]

Two such non-wage aspects—job security and (at least in the federal sector) pensions—appear to be very attractive in government compared to the private sector. Failure to consider this would seem, *a priori*, to produce public wage rates that are higher than necessary to attract an adequate work force.

3) Prior to the advent of collective bargaining in the public service, governments had exhibited a tendency to dispense with their adherence to the prevailing wage principle whenever the need to economize arose, since public service wages were often the easiest target.[9] Partly for this reason, public sector wage scales prior to the 1960s may have lagged behind the private sector. In recent years, however, it is generally believed that public sector employees have caught up with and even surpassed their private sector counterparts in terms of wage compensation, while maintaining their non-wage advantages. Evidence to support or refute this view can be obtained from a comparison of wage and fringe benefits won in the public sector relative to comparable private sector employment. If employees in the public sector consistently fare better now than comparable employees in the private sector, this would tend to support the view that current legislation has tilted the balance of bargaining power too much in the public employees' favour.

11

C. WAGE AND SALARY COMPARISONS

The source most often cited when public/private wage comparisons are wanted has been the annual percentage base wage increases compiled by Labour Canada from collective agreements covering 500 or more employees. These figures are presented in Table 5, for 1967 through 1976. They show the annual percentage increases in base wage rates separately for the private sector and various components of the public sector. It is clear from the Table that percentage increases in the public sector were generally somewhat lower than those in the private sector until 1972, but that from 1973 on public sector increases have exceeded increases in the private sector. The higher increases in the public sector for this latter period, and particularly the exceptionally large increases for 1975, are probably responsible for much of the current negative reaction to public sector settlements.

Comparisons using base wage rate data can be misleading

However, although they are popular, these figures can be seriously misleading. The base rate data used refer only to the rate paid to the lowest job classification for workers in the bargaining unit. Most employees in the bargaining unit will be working in a job classification which is above the base rate. Hence, the figures reported by Labour Canada do not refer to increases in *actual* wages received by most workers. Because a given increase in the base rate causes a corresponding increase in the rate paid for all higher job classifications, the base rate increases reported by Labour Canada could provide a reasonably accurate comparison of wage gains in the public and private sectors if movement through the job classification structure were comparable between the two sectors. But this is unlikely to be the case. Percentage increases in base rates are less meaningful as a measure of the employees' annual salary increase in the public sector than in the private sector, since public sector employees are regularly promoted through a step system of job classification which is accompanied by salary increments in addition to the base rate increases. Hence, the wage gains presented in Table 5 could substantially under-estimate the actual wage gains made in the public sector.

On the other hand, there is a large and growing proportion of employees in the private sector with provision for cost of living adjustments, which are not included in the base rate calculations.[10] Adjustment for the implementation of cost of living provisions could substantially reduce the disparity between average public and private base rate percentage increases in the Table. The end result is that it is not clear whether public sector employees have been winning larger per-centage wage increases than private sector workers, and even if that could be established, that would not resolve the real issue which concerns the *level* of public sector wages compared to the private sector.

Comparisons using actual earnings

A better picture of the relationship between public and private sector wages and salaries can be obtained by looking at *actual* earnings for employees in each sector. In a study for the Institute for Research on Public Policy, Morley Gunderson used tax return data to compute average earnings per employee in the private sector and in various components of the public sector, for 1946 through 1975. These data are presented in Table 6, as the ratio of public to private sector average earnings. As the last column of Table 6 indicates, average earnings in the public sector tended to fall short of those in the private sector until the mid-1960s. Since that time (during which unionization developed rapidly in the public sector), public sector earnings have exceeded those in the private sector. As the separate columns show, the growth of public sector earnings relative to those in the private sector has occurred in all parts of the public sector, with the most rapid gains being made by teachers and federal government employees. Hence, these data would seem to support the popular opinion that most public sector employees have sur-passed wage parity with the private sector.

13

Indications that public sector employees enjoy an earnings advantage over private sector employees are even stronger when consideration is taken of public/private sector differences in the length of the typical work-week and work-year. Data published annually by Labour Canada in *Working Conditions in Canadian Industry* show that public sector employees typically work fewer hours per week and enjoy more paid holidays per year than employees in the private sector. Adjustment for this would raise the "real" earnings differential between public and private sector employees above the values presented in Table 6.

There is an additional reason for caution in the interpretation of the figures in Table 6. To quote Gunderson:

"...the actual value of the ratio in any given year does not tell us much about public/private sector earnings differences for a given type of labour, since the earnings figures are for all different types of employees. A high ratio of government/business earnings, for example, may reflect a higher embodiment of human capital in government employees; it may even be consistent with the government sector paying lower wages for comparable work performed in the private sector."[11]

The consistent increase in the ratio of public to private sector earnings over the years may reflect an increase in the average level of qualification required for public sector jobs relative to the private sector, rather than the appearance of a wage advantage in the public sector for a given job skill. Indeed, evidence from the 1971 Census does indicate that the average education of government employees exceeds that of employees in the private sector.[12] What we cannot tell from these data is whether the differences in the qualifications of public employees relative to those in the private sector are sufficient to fully justify the earnings advantage of the public sector.

Ideally, the data we would like in order to determine whether public sector pay rates are comparable to those in the private sector are public and private wages and salaries actually paid, by type of job. At least for the federal sector, the Pay Research Bureau collects these data. Unfortunately, however, the data made available to the public by the Bureau describe only the minimum and maximum rates of pay potentially obtainable for each type of job in the public sector. Publication of rates paid in the public sector is not permitted at this time because it would violate confidentiality requirements by identifying the rates paid by a single employer—usually the Treasury Board. Consequently, data from the Pay Research Bureau are not of much use to us in making public/private pay comparisons. There are other avenues open to us though.

Comparisons using rates of pay by occupation

A rough comparison of the level of pay scales by occupation between the private sector and the public sector can be made by using the results of the annual survey made by Labour Canada on wage rates, salaries, and hours of labour. This survey is taken in October of each year, and collects wage and salary data, by industry and occupation, for 37 of the largest cities across Canada. A time series of such data was compiled by Gunderson, for the labourer occupation only, for 1952 through 1973. These data are presented in Table 7. The figures are easiest to interpret by focusing on the last line, which shows a ratio, defined as the wage paid to a municipal labourer divided by the wage paid to a labourer in the private sector, averaged over all cities in the sample. Thus, in 1950, labourers working for municipalities received only 93 per cent of the wage received by labourers in the private sector, on average. By 1973, the municipal wage for labourers had increased to 109 per cent of the wage received by labourers in the private sector. The public sector wage advantage first appeared in 1960 and has grown steadily since then. Hence, to the extent that the experience of labourers is representative of other occupational categories, these data support popular opinion concerning the pattern of public/private sector wage differentials over time. However, although the data do permit

15

a comparison of *actual* wages paid, by specific type of job, these figures, too, could be subject to criticism for several reasons.

The most obvious criticism is that the figures refer to only one type of job, and hence, can provide no assurance that a similar public sector wage advantage exists for other types of jobs. In addition, considering the dispute at the federal level between the Treasury Board and public employee unions concerning the relevant universe in which to determine the prevailing wage, it might be expected that employee groups would object to the comparisons contained in Table 7, because the private sector comparison is the average wage in all employer establishments, regardless of their size or extent of unionization. Employee groups might maintain that a more appropriate comparison would be between the public sector and those larger establishments in the private sector which are unionized.

Comparisons by size and unionization of employing establishment

In an attempt to deal with these shortcomings in the figures in Table 7, we have compiled additional data from the same survey which permit a more detailed comparison of public/ private sector wage and salary differentials. These figures are presented in Table 8. They are taken from the October, 1974, survey on wage rates, salaries, and hours of labour. This is the only year used because it is the first year in which the survey results show wage and salary figures broken down by size and unionization of the employing establishment, and because it is the last year for which data are available that are free of the distortions probably introduced by wage and price controls. We present wage or salary comparisons for four job categories: male labourer, female file clerk, female administrative manager, and male administrative manager. Although the 1974 survey covered 35 cities, in only five cities was the sample size large enough to present data separately for public administration, and thus to permit the public/private comparisons.

16

These data, too, support the popular opinion that public sector employees have surpassed wage parity with the private sector. In every city for which data are available, public sector file clerks were paid a higher weekly salary than private sector file clerks; the length of the public sector work week was as short or shorter than the work week in the private sector as well. The same advantageous situation exists for public sector labourers as compared to private sector labourers with the single exception of Regina, where public sector labourers were paid less (for a shorter work week) than their private sector counterparts. Even the data for managers, where it might be expected that the typical private sector manager shoulders more responsibility than the typical public sector manager, show that the public sector pays about as well or better than the private sector. In fact, females in high level jobs in the public sector appear to fare considerably better than they do in the private sector, probably as the result of the government having assumed the moral obligation to pay the "fair" rather than the market-determined wage to members of those groups which are popularly thought to be at a disadvantage in the labour market. Even when compared to union pay scales in the private sector, or to pay scales in establishments with 500 or more employees, the pay scales in the public sector are generally higher. (See the figures in parentheses in Table 8.)

Thus, although we cannot obtain the ideal comparison we would like, of actual wages paid for a wide variety of corresponding jobs in the public and the private sectors, the imperfect comparisons that we have been able to make from published tabulations all support the view that, while public sector wage and salary compensation may have once lagged behind the private sector, since the 1960s public sector employees have attained and even surpassed parity with private sector employees in comparable jobs. The determinants of this earnings differential in favour of public sector employees have been investigated econometrically in a second, more recent study by Gunderson.

17

Determinants of the public/private sector earnings differential

Using data from the 1971 Canadian Census, Gunderson estimated separate earnings equations for public and private (manufacturing) sector employees. He used these equations to decompose the average public/private sector earnings differential into two parts: one part is consistent with the prevailing wage principle, since it is due to the higher average quality of public sector employees as measured by education, experience, job skill, etc.; the other part, which presumably measures the pure surplus or economic rent accruing to employees in the public sector, is not consistent with the prevailing wage principle. Gunderson's results are reproduced in Table 9.

Gunderson found an overall average earnings advantage for public sector male employees of 9.3 per cent. After eliminating from this that portion of the differential which could be justified by differences in qualification between private and public sector employees in the sample, an earnings differential of 6.2 per cent still remains.

Gunderson found an overall average earnings advantage for public sector female employees of 22.3 per cent. After eliminating from this that portion of the differential which could be justified by differences in qualification between private and public sector employees in the sample, an earnings differential of 8.6 per cent still remains.

Further analysis of the earnings equations estimated by Gunderson separately for the public and private sectors shows that "the public sector tends to pay its surplus wage payment in the form of a constant wage advantage rather than in the form of an excessive premium for the acquisition of wage-generating characteristics."[13] In other words, regardless of education, experience, or job skill, earnings are likely to increase by a constant mark-up when an employee moves from a private sector job to a comparable job in the public sector. As a result, the public sector earnings advantage, in percentage terms, is greater for low-level jobs than it is for high-level jobs.

18

Having found strong statistical evidence of a six to eight per cent wage mark-up in the public sector relative to wages received by comparable private sector employees, Gunderson goes on to say,

> "There are theoretical reasons to suggest that these magnitudes may understate the true advantage in total compensation associated with public sector employment. Specifically, the possibility exists that public sector employees have better fringe benefits and greater job security. These factors may be more prevalent in the public sector because political administrations may try to save on current wage costs by granting deferred wages in the form of job security and liberal retirement and pension schemes."[14]

We turn to an examination of this issue in the following section.

D. NON-WAGE COMPARISONS

As indicated earlier, both efficiency and equity require that public sector employees receive compensation comparable to that received by those in the private sector doing comparable work. However, the relevant measure of compensation is not wages and salaries alone, but rather total compensation, which considers wages, fringe benefits, job security, and working conditions. In the preceding section, we have seen evidence which indicates that, in terms of wages and salaries alone, public sector employees now fare better than private sector employees doing comparable work. If this wage advantage were offset by lesser non-wage benefits in the public relative to the private sector, overall public/private parity might exist nevertheless. However, the meagre evidence that is available on this issue appears to indicate that the public sector provides non-wage benefits that, for most employees, are as good as or better than those available in the private sector, so that the earnings advantage we have found for public sector employees carries over to an advantage in total compensation as well.

19

Fringe benefits

What evidence there is on which to base this conclusion has been summarized by Gunderson, in his previously cited study. The best documented evidence is that concerning the value of fringe benefits in the municipal and provincial public sectors relative to those in the private sectors. We have reproduced Gunderson's data on these values in Table 10. The data in this Table show that, although there are variations in the distribution among various types of fringe benefits, the overall value of fringe benefits is roughly comparable for employees in the non-federal public and the private sectors.

Again, due to the requirements of confidentiality, there are no corresponding figures published by the Pay Research Bureau for the federal sector. In an unpublished 1977 conference report, D. Morley claims that "as far as fringe benefits are concerned...we [the federal sector] are comparable with the average level of benefits provided by outside employers."[15] But when it is considered that federal public employees are virtually unique in their entitlement to full escalation of their pension benefits based on the Consumer Price Index, it seems likely that, at least in periods of high inflation such as we have experienced over the last decade, the overall present value of fringe benefits available to federal public employees exceeds that available to private sector employees.[16]

Job security and working conditions

Evidence concerning job security and working conditions, the final components of total compensation, is the most difficult to obtain. It is certainly the common belief that the public sector, at all levels, is characterized by greater job security and easier working conditions than are typical in the private sector. Gunderson says that "it is true that permanent employees have a reasonable degree of *employment* security once in the public sector," but "there is no guarantee that they will remain in the particular *job* of their choice."[17] Further, Gunderson claims that, for some individuals, the private sector has some off-setting benefits, principally in the form of the greater prevalence of overtime, and of the opportunity to obtain an extremely high executive salary for those willing to take risks.[18] Indeed, two recent studies have documented a private sector salary advantage at the most senior executive levels.[19] This, however, applies to only a small fraction of all public sector employees.

E. SUMMARY OF COMPENSATION COMPARISONS

In summary, investigation leads to the conclusion that, for all but the most senior executive employees, the total compensation package typical for public sector employees is more generous than the compensation available to private sector employees doing comparable work. The public sector advantage with respect to wages and salaries is in the order of six to eight per cent, after eliminating pay differences which could be justified by differences in qualifications. With respect to fringe benefits, the evidence seems to indicate that public sector employees do at least as well as those in the private sector, and that federal sector public employees may do considerably better than private sector employees in terms of pension benefits during periods of inflation. Comparisons with respect to job security and working conditions are difficult to make, but the presumption is that both are more favourable in the public sector, at all levels, than in the private sector.

The implication of this evidence is that the government is not just a "good" employer; it has become one of the "best" employers in the economy. While the logic of the prevailing wage principle implies that the public sector should take its lead from private sector compensation packages, Canada in recent years has seen the reversal of this principle, so that now private sector employees are pointing to gains made in the public sector to justify their bargaining demands. Further, the pay advantage now enjoyed by public sector employees arose simultaneously with the rise of public sector unionism. This, in itself, does not prove that current legislation is too permissive regarding union activity in the public sector, but it does offer considerable support to that view.

CHAPTER THREE

Public Sector
Labour Relations Policy

In Canada, and in the countries whose policies often serve as a model for Canadian policies, union activity in the public sector has traditionally been subject to more severe constraints than those generally applicable to the private sector. But recently Canadian public sector labour relations policies have diverged radically from those of her principal models, the United States and Britain. In the mid-1960s, federal and most provincial labour legislation in Canada was changed to permit greater scope for legal union activity in the public sector. Wages were made subject to collective bargaining everywhere, and the strike weapon was made legally available to many public sector workers. This contrasts sharply with policy in the United States, where all federal and most state government workers are prohibited from striking and are not permitted to bargain over wages (although they may bargain over working conditions). It also contrasts with policy in Britain, where wages in public administration are normally determined not by bargaining, but rather by strict adherence to private sector comparability guidelines. Canadian public sector labour relations policy is now among the most liberal in the world. Despite the liberalization, there remain significant differences between labour policy for the private and public sectors. Further, there are differences among the federal and the 10

23

provincial jurisdictions in labour relations policy toward their public employees. There are even differences within a province in the way that provincial employees are governed compared to the way that municipal employees are governed by labour legislation.

COLLECTIVE BARGAINING LEGISLATION BY JURISDICTION

Table 11 summarizes some of the differences among jurisdictions in labour relations policy toward public employees. In order to describe labour relations policy in the public sector, it is helpful to break public employees down into five groups—civil servants, teachers, police, firefighters, and hospital workers.

In all provinces, municipalities are considered to be corporations under private sector law and, as such, their labour relations are governed by the labour legislation relevant to private sector employees unless provision for the exclusion of certain employee groups is made by special provincial legislation. Those municipal employees often excluded from coverage under private sector labour legislation are police and firefighters.

Those municipal employees who are governed by private sector labour legislation are guaranteed the right to organize and bargain collectively, to be represented by a certified union, to enter into binding collective agreements which are enforceable through conventional grievance procedures and adjudication, and to engage in legal strikes.

With the exception of the armed forces and the federal police (the RCMP), who are denied the right to bargain collectively, federal and provincial public employees in every jurisdiction are also guaranteed the right to organize, to bargain collectively, to be represented by a certified union, and to enter into binding collective agreements which are enforceable through conventional grievance procedures and adjudication. However, in most jurisdictions there are

24

statutory limits on the issues which are subject to collective bargaining. This limitation is partly the result of the imposition of a system of collective bargaining onto an already existing civil service system at both the federal and provincial levels. More fundamentally, however, it has its justification in the need to maintain the quality and the flexibility of the government work force.

LIMITATIONS ON THE SCOPE OF BARGAINING

Under the merit principles of the civil service system, the relevant public service commission had and continues to have the authority to make appointments, transfers, promotions, demotions, and layoffs. These are not legitimately within the scope of negotiations permitted for civil servants although the collective bargain may contain provisions regarding the financial impact of unfavourable job actions (such as severance pay). In many jurisdictions, superannuation benefits are also excluded from the legitimate scope of bargaining. This limitation on bargaining is one of several which might be eliminated without further serious detriment to the operational efficiency of the public service by the introduction of a "two-tier" system of bargaining, as explained later. There are a number of issues, such as hiring standards, promotion standards, classification procedures, health and pension benefits, which should be uniform throughout each (federal or provincial) public service if the public employer is to retain the flexibility to deploy his work force efficiently. Most jurisdictions have dealt with this need by deciding these issues unilaterally, either within the public service commission or legislatively.

However, the scope of public sector bargaining could be widened to include at least some of these issues if the several bargaining units within the public service would combine to bargain jointly on those issues which should be uniform service-wide, while continuing to bargain separately on those issues which are specific to their membership. Two-tier bar-

25

gaining of this sort is already practiced in some provincial jurisdictions; British Columbia is an example. Some change along these lines has been approved, in principle, but not yet implemented for the federal public service as well.[20]

LIMITATIONS ON THE RIGHT TO STRIKE

In addition to limits on the scope of bargaining, the various jurisdictions impose differing degrees of restriction on the right of public employees to engage in strikes. The provinces of British Columbia and Saskatchewan are the most liberal of the jurisdictions. In these provinces, all public employees, with the single exception of public school teachers, have the legal right to strike. By special legislation, teachers in British Columbia and Saskatchewan submit their negotiation disputes to binding arbitration; this restriction on the right to strike for teachers was passed with their strong support. In both Saskatchewan and British Columbia, police and firefighters are encouraged to resolve their disputes in negotiations via binding arbitration, though they have the ultimate right to strike. In British Columbia, provision is made for hospital workers to opt for binding arbitration as well.

The provinces of New Brunswick, Newfoundland, and Quebec are only slightly more restrictive in their public sector labour relations. While most public employees in these provinces have the ultimate right to strike, this right is denied to police and firefighters. In Newfoundland, the strike is denied to hospital workers as well. Their negotiation disputes must be submitted to binding arbitration for resolution .

The remaining five provinces—Alberta, Manitoba, Nova Scotia, Ontario, and Prince Edward Island—are the most restrictive concerning public sector strikes. Civil servants in these provinces may not lawfully engage in strikes; disputes are resolved by binding arbitration. However, treatment of the other public employee groups varies among the provinces. In Prince Edward Island, no public employees have the right to strike. In Ontario, police, firefighters, and hospital workers

26

must resort to arbitration to resolve an impasse in negotiations, but teachers are ultimately free to strike. In Nova Scotia, teachers may resort to the strike on certain issues. Police, firefighters, and hospital workers are governed by private sector legislation and are consequently unrestricted in their right to strike, at least in principle. Manitoba provides for binding arbitration to resolve negotiation disputes for teachers, police, and firefighters, but hospital workers are governed by private sector legislation, with its unrestricted right to strike. Alberta provides binding arbitration for police and firefighters, but permits teachers and hospital workers to strike.

It should be noted that all provinces which permit the strike to any of their public employees have various options available to them in the event a strike endangers the public. For example, in Alberta, strikes may be terminated by order of the cabinet under the general "emergency" provisions of the private sector labour code, if the situation warrants such action. In British Columbia, there is legislative provision for the cabinet to order a cooling-off period not to exceed 40 days when any imminent or existing work stoppage poses an immediate and serious danger to life or health; in the case of police, firefighters, and hospital workers, the prescribed cooling-off period may be as long as 90 days, with the possibility of one 14-day extension. Beyond that, most jurisdictions have legislative provision for the labour relations board to designate services that it considers necessary or essential to prevent immediate and serious danger to life, health, or safety which must continue to be provided, in the event of a strike, by the unions. Finally, all jurisdictions may ultimately resort to *ad hoc* legislation to terminate a strike.

THE FEDERAL JURISDICTION

Labour relations policy in the federal public service is similar to that in the more liberal of the provinces. Pursuant to the *Public Service Staff Relations Act,* passed in 1967, most federal public service employees have the right to organize and

27

to bargain collectively. Only those employees working in a managerial or confidential capacity are excluded from the benefits of the legislation.[21] However, as in the provinces, a number of issues are outside the legitimate scope of negotiations permitted by the Act. Old age, death, and disability benefits in the federal public service are governed by separate statute and are therefore not negotiable. Further, the *Public Service Employment Act* confers upon the Public Service Commission the authority to govern the appointment, appraisal, promotion, demotion, transfer, and release of employees, so that these too are outside the scope of negotiations permitted by the *Public Service Staff Relations Act.* As already mentioned, a two-tier system of bargaining might permit the legitimate scope of negotiations to be broadened without serious further detriment to the operational efficiency of the public service.

The right to strike in the federal public service is dependent on the process specified for the resolution of any dispute at the time the bargaining agent is certified by the Public Service Staff Relations Board. Each bargaining unit may opt for either arbitration or conciliation in order to resolve disputes. If arbitration is selected, it is binding on both parties and a work stoppage is forbidden. If conciliation is chosen, the strike is permitted once the conciliation process has been completed. The bargaining unit may later change its chosen procedure for dispute settlement, but the change will be effective only for subsequent, not ongoing, negotiations.

It is significant that the initial recommendations for collective bargaining in the federal public service specified only binding arbitration, not the strike, in the event of an impasse in negotiations. However, the illegal strike by postal workers in 1965 impressed upon the government some hard realities: 1) public sector employees were coming to believe that they were entitled to the same privileges enjoyed by private sector workers, including the right to strike; 2) many public sector workers were prepared to strike illegally, if necessary; and 3) it is difficult, if not impossible, to dismiss or impose other meaningful sanctions on employees who have engaged in an illegal work stoppage when support for the action is widespread. Hence, the legislation, when proclaimed in 1967, provided for either arbitration or conciliation (with the strike implicit) in the event of an impasse in negotiations.[22]

Those units which choose the conciliation option may be limited in their right to strike. Prior to the start of negotiations, the employer and the union must agree on a list of employees or classes of employees whose duties are essential to the safety or security of the public. If the two parties cannot agree on this list, the Public Service Staff Relations Board is authorized to make the final determination. Employees on this list are termed "designated" employees; only non-designated employees may go on strike. Thus, the law provides for a partial strike, and it is up to the Board to decide on the degree, which could, in principle, range all the way from no strike to a total strike.[23]

CHAPTER FOUR

Bargaining in the Federal Public Service

At the time the *Public Service Staff Relations Act* was passed, it was assumed that the majority of employees would choose binding arbitration rather than the strike as the final step for resolving negotiation disputes. That assumption proved to be correct initially. In March 1970, more than 75 per cent of the federal employees covered by collective bargaining had opted for binding arbitration. However, since that time, there have been numerous changes in dispute settlement specifications. As a result of these changes, more than two-thirds of the employees covered by collective bargaining in the federal public service are now in bargaining units for which the conciliation/strike option has been specified as the dispute settlement process.[24] The magnitude of this turnaround would seem to indicate some problem with the arbitration process in the federal jurisdiction. Since either voluntary or compulsory arbitration of public sector disputes is a common feature in the provincial jurisdictions as well, analysis of the problems in the federal arbitration process is of broad interest.

REASONS FOR THE SHIFT FROM ARBITRATION TO THE STRIKE OPTION

No doubt some of the reasons for the massive switch from the arbitration to the conciliation/strike option in the federal public service are largely unrelated to the effectiveness with which the arbitration system has operated. New attitudes associated with the influx of younger employees into the public service and the pressures exerted by private sections of the trade union movement to join the mainstream would probably have resulted in some drift towards the conciliation/strike option regardless of other factors. Further, some initial preference for arbitration, followed by a growing preference for the strike, is a natural response to the economic circumstances of the time.

"During the early years of bargaining, a 'catch-up' in wages, fringe benefits, and contractual language occurred. Bargaining in these years was characterized by a rapid diffusion of benefits and contract provisions across the various bargaining units. This pattern setting and following process (reinforced by the use of internal relativity comparisons by arbitrators) meant that the majority of units could benefit from choosing the arbitration route than from threatening or actually engaging in a work stoppage...[By 1975, however,] most of the differentials in benefits and other contract provisions had been eliminated and any new gains required breaking new ground [which is better accomplished via conciliation /strike than via arbitration] rather than catching up to other units in the system."[25]

Nevertheless, it is the opinion of most analysts in the area that the main reason for the growing preference for the conciliation/strike option is that the arbitration system has not functioned as well as it could have. To be viable, a system of voluntary arbitration must ensure that, overall, the needs and demands of employees are met as effectively under that system as under the conciliation/strike system. This does not seem to be the case in the federal system. A number of factors have contributed to dissatisfaction with the arbitration option among federal public service employees:[26]

1) Limitation on items which are arbitrable

The scope of the issues that can be resolved by arbitration has been (*de facto*, if not *de jure*) more limited than those that will be dealt with by a conciliation board. By law, no collective agreement in the federal public service may include any provision that would require the enactment or amendment of any legislation by Parliament, except for the purpose of appropriating the money required for its implementation. Further, no collective agreement may contain any provision concerning the standards, procedures, or processes governing the appointment, promotion, demotion, transfer, layoff, or release of employees. Hence, at first glance, both the conciliation and the arbitration routes seem to be equally restricted in terms of the issues they may resolve. However, the *Public Service Staff Relations Act* goes on to specify those particular issues that an arbitral award *may* cover: rates of pay, hours of work, leave entitlements, standards of discipline, and other terms and conditions of employment directly related thereto. Arbitration boards have given a strict interpretation to this last provision, refusing to make any judgement on issues which do not seem to fit within the specified allowable categories.

Conciliation boards, however, have taken a more flexible approach. Conciliation boards are generally willing to make recommendations on any issues which have not been specifically *excluded* by law from the collective bargain. Further, in contrast to arbitration boards, conciliation boards have been willing to devote time to seeking formulae on various matters that cannot lawfully be included in the collective agreement, but that the employer may, nevertheless, be willing to discuss with his employees in the interest of promoting good labour relations. The narrow and legalistic approach taken under arbitration, compared to the more flexible approach followed under conciliation, is particularly undesirable given the requirement that employee bargaining agents specify whether they will use the arbitration or the conciliation route prior to the start of negotiations. The result is that those agents which

32

choose arbitration have, in effect, notified the employer that there are certain issues which he can, with impunity, refuse to negotiate, although those same issues would have been subject to negotiation had conciliation been chosen instead.

One very desirable amendment to the *Public Service Staff Relations Act* would permit the union's bargaining agent to specify the arbitration or the conciliation/strike route at the time of an impasse in negotiations, rather than at the start of negotiations. This is the current practice in public sector bargaining in New Brunswick. This is a more realistic approach to the resolution of disputes, since it permits the bargaining agent to choose the method of impasse resolution after he has determined the nature of the issues which cannot be resolved by the parties themselves. Arbitration is well suited to the resolution of disputes which are simple, black-or-white issues; conciliation is preferable when the dispute requires some innovation for resolution. In addition, this amendment would eliminate one of the major disadvantages to the arbitration choice, since it eliminates the incentive for the employer to refuse to bargain on certain, non-arbitrable issues once he knows that the employees have opted for arbitration. The argument against this is that the process of determining which employees should be designated in the interests of safety and security may take weeks, and that if this were delayed to the point of impasse, employees might become increasingly restless. This problem could be easily resolved, though, if there were consultation and agreement on designation prior to the commencement of bargaining, in the event that an impasse and a strike do ensue.

More direct action could be taken to reduce current union dissatisfaction with the arbitration option by broadening the scope of arbitration to include all those issues which are negotiable. The public service unions are, of course, strongly in favour of this. However, J. Finkelman, chairman of the Public Service Staff Relations Board, has recommended against it. Finkelman argues that:

33

"when the end process for resolution of disputes is the strike weapon, the employee organization concerned must make hard-nosed compromises between the claims of conflicting groups in light of the risks involved. If everything bargainable is also arbitrable, there are no risks, or only very minimal risks, involved in throwing every issue, no matter how insignificant it may be, into the lap of the arbitrator. There is no inducement to the leadership of an organization to resist political pressure and it is therefore all the more likely to yield to the wishes of every small group of employees...The result could be chaotic not only because of the intolerable burden that would be cast on the arbitration mechanism, but also because it would negate the fundamental philosophy of a collective bargaining system, which is that an agreement entered into by the parties themselves is vastly superior to an award forced on them by a third party..."[27]

Moreover, Finkelman goes on to argue that because current legislation subjects the federal employer to arbitration at the sole option of the bargaining agent, federal public sector unions have an additional alternative, not available to most unions in the private sector. This enormously strengthens the bargaining position of those units whose employees, because of the nature of their work, cannot bring pressure to bear upon the employer by the withdrawal of services. Finkelman sees the limitation on the scope of arbitration as a means of restoring, to a degree, the balance of employee-employer power in bargaining.[28] While there is merit to Finkelman's arguments, it should be noted that the imbalance in employee-employer power created by the arbitration selection procedure can be more logically corrected by making arbitration available only on agreement of *both* parties, as is the current practice in public sector bargaining in New Brunswick. Further, Finkelman himself argues elsewhere that:

"if there is a wide discrepancy between items bargainable and items arbitrable, the employees in some bargaining units that have so far been content to live under the arbitration option might in the future be impelled to specify the conciliation board option, i.e., they might choose the strike route, a result that one cannot view with equanimity. In short, if resort to arbitration is to be regarded . . . as a preferable course for dispute settlement, a balance must be maintained between what may be achieved through resort to either of the processes.''[29]

In light of the recent realization of his fears, this passage would seem to indicate that even Finkelman might now be willing to advocate broadening of the scope of arbitration.

2) Selection procedure for members of the arbitration board

A second disadvantage to arbitration in the federal public sector, compared to the conciliation option, is that the parties have little influence in the selection of the members of the arbitration board. The arbitration board members are selected by the Public Service Staff Relations Board from an existing panel of employer and employee representatives. By contrast, the members of a conciliation board consist of an appointee of each party, freely chosen, and a mutually selected chairman. Thus, the members of a conciliation board are likely to be better informed about, and hence better qualified to resolve, the particular issues in dispute. It may well be desirable to have the chairman of an arbitration board selected from an experienced group within the Public Service Staff Relations Board, in order to better assure consistency in arbitral awards. However, there seems to be no strong argument to support the current denial of choice of board representatives to those parties choosing arbitration, while those parties choosing conciliation are unrestricted.

3) Inadequate explanation of rationale behind arbitration awards

A third disadvantage to arbitration, compared to conciliation, is that arbitration boards have typically refused to offer any explanation of the rationale on which their award is based. By contrast, the recommendations of a conciliation board are accompanied by explanatory material, as they must be if they are to persuade both sides that the recommendations are fair and worthy of acceptance. The *Public Service Staff Relations Act* specifies the factors that the arbitration board should take into consideration, but without specific information from the arbitration board about the weights they attached to the various factors and the comparisons they considered relevant, it is not surprising that the fairness of some arbitration awards is questioned. It should be noted that there have been proposals recently to remedy this by amending the *Public Service Staff Relations Act* to require that arbitral awards be accompanied by the reasons which underlie the decision reached. (See footnote 21.)

Hence, even if the basic framework of the *Public Service Staff Relations Act* is retained, there are some amendments to the Act which could help to place the choice of arbitration on a more equal footing with the conciliation/strike option, with a resultant benefit to the public in terms of fewer disruptions of public services. Similar considerations may also apply at the provincial level. However, a more fundamental issue concerns the distinction between public sector and private sector, and whether the current trend toward the elimination of differences in labour policy between the two sectors should continue, or be reversed. This issue is discussed in the following chapter.

CHAPTER FIVE

Bargaining Problems Specific to the Public Sector

It is understandable that public employees, like their private sector counterparts, should have developed interest in some form of unionism and collective bargaining. After all, the basic labour relations problem is the same for private and public employment. Whether in the public or the private sector, employer-employee conflicts are going to arise concerning compensation, advancement, discipline, supervision, and a host of other issues affecting the work environment. Public employees have as much cause to suspect uninhibited decision-making by their administrative superiors as have their counterparts in private employment.

THE ROLE OF THE PUBLIC SERVICE COMMISSION

Until the advent of collective bargaining in their public sectors, labour relations matters were dealt with in the federal and provincial jurisdictions by a civil service or public service commission. The commission served a dual purpose, performing personnel functions for the employer by recruiting, appointing, and assigning employees, while serving also as an adjudicator for employees with grievances against their employer. Salary scales were set by the appropriate legislature on the recommendation of the commission, which based its recommendations on the salaries necessary to attract employees of sufficient quality and number from the private sector.

While the public service commission is designed, in part, as a substitute for the union protection available to employees in the private sector, it suffers from the belief by employees that it is too closely linked to the public employer, and hence cannot fairly perform its function of adjudicating employee grievances. The collective bargaining framework has come to be viewed as a preferable mechanism for resolving employee grievances, as well as a means of winning larger pay increases than would be recommended by the public service commission.

In the early 1960s, the Diefenbaker government attempted to satisfy the demands of federal public service employees for a greater role in the determination of their pay and working conditions by introducing a formalized system of consultation with employee representatives. However, this only resulted in an intensified demand for full-scale collective bargaining by public service employees when it became evident that the government intended to treat these consultative rights "as a hollow ritual which was to have chiefly a propaganda value."[30]

As a result, more and more of the bargaining privileges which private sector workers have had for years are gradually being granted to workers in the public sector as well. The current trend clearly indicates the erosion of the sphere of influence of the public service commission. It is losing its role as protector of the interests of public employees to the unions, and, consequently, it is becoming more unambiguous as simply the personnel office for the public employer.

THE PUBLIC/PRIVATE VS. THE ESSENTIALITY CRITERION

The distinction in labour relations policy between public and private sectors is becoming blurred, while a new distinction is emerging—that between "essential" workers or services, whose withdrawal cannot be tolerated by the public, and all other workers whose participation in work stoppages may inconvenience, but not endanger, the public. It is our purpose to argue that there are good reasons for labour relations policy to distinguish not only between essential workers and others, but also between public and private sector workers.

It is important to note that "essential" services may be provided either in the public or the private sector. Police and fire protection are examples of services generally considered essential in the public sector; hospital and transport services are examples of services often considered essential which may be provided either publicly or privately.

Unfortunately, the essentiality criterion is a good deal more ambiguous than the public/private criterion which has been so important in labour policy in the past. Even in the private sector, the question of when a strike constitutes a genuine emergency has never been resolved with finality.

> "The reason is not that an emergency cannot be defined in a way that will satisfy informed opinion, but rather that the public inevitably finds such a definition too narrow. Indeed, many of the cases of *ad hoc* intervention...have not involved disputes that were, strictly speaking, emergencies. The political pressures surrounding strikes that are severely inconvenient but not dangerous are such that strict obedience to the criterion of actual emergency would involve too great a political risk..."[31]

The situation in the public sector is still more difficult. Most strikes in the public sector—all those worth staging—inconvenience a substantial part of the community. If there is not to be a total ban on strikes by public employees, political adherence to a distinction between true emergencies and real inconvenience is necessary. Otherwise we run the risk of creating tremendous labour unrest by establishing, via *ad hoc* legislation, the precedent of the occasional arbitrary withdrawal of the right to strike from selected employee groups depending only on the public temper at the time. The

39

circumstances surrounding Parliament's termination of the postal workers' strike at the end of 1978 are indicative. Consequently, it seems desirable that the discretion to determine whether an emergency exists be delegated to an independent, administrative tribunal rather than to elected public officials who will be politically unable to apply the distinction. The appropriate agency to make the determination would probably be the relevant labour relations board.

"ESSENTIAL" SERVICES

Little need be said concerning the prohibition of work stoppages by workers providing "essential" services. Clearly, where a strike, whether in the public or private sector, creates an immediate danger to public health or safety, the strike should be outlawed and resort to prescribed post-impasse procedures made mandatory. Such policy would seem to be appropriate for police and firefighters in all jurisdictions. The few instances in Canada and the United States of work stoppages by police have shown that widespread looting and property damage are the immediate result, unless alternative forces are quickly moved into place. There is tremendous potential for loss of life and property if firefighters should refuse to respond to an alarm. For these reasons, a total strike by police or firefighters is always an emergency situation. As indicated in Table 11, most jurisdictions in Canada provide for compulsory arbitration rather than the strike to resolve negotiation disputes with these workers; but even those jurisdictions that have no existing prohibition against strikes by police and firefighters have shown that they will quickly resort to *ad hoc* legislation should a work stoppage among these workers threaten.

However, though not currently practiced in any jurisdiction, some labour relations experts have suggested that even such essential employees may be permitted to engage in strictly limited work stoppages, as a means of venting the frustration and anger which are bound to arise on occasion during the course of collective bargaining *before* relations have soured to

40

such an extent that an illegal and total work stoppage occurs with its consequent threat to public safety. For example, the police might continue to patrol and to respond to emergency calls, but refuse to direct traffic, issue citations, appear in court, or do the administrative paperwork that is also a part of their responsibilities. Such limited work stoppages are enough to bring the attention of the public to the problems being encountered by the employees, while not enough to endanger the public. They can serve as a useful escape valve for essential employees. By contrast, if frustrations are allowed to mount until a total strike by essential employees results, major sanctions must be imposed on the striking employees in order to protect the public by dissuading any further such actions. These major sanctions may include dismissal of the striking employees, heavy fines or imprisonment of employees or their union officials, and decertification of the union representing the employees. The former alternative of the limited work stoppage seems clearly preferable.

In other situations, where the length of the strike determines the magnitude of the threat to the public, a less restrictive approach could be taken. For example, a strike by hospital workers or sanitation workers may be tolerable for a time. But the longer it continues, the greater is the threat to public health. In such instances, there need not be a blanket prohibition of total strikes, but there should be some agent empowered by standing legislation to determine whether an emergency exists and, if so, to order the termination of the strike and to invoke appropriate post-impasse procedures. As indicated earlier, the relevant labour relations board seems the appropriate agent.

OTHER PUBLIC SERVICES

However, most of those employed in the public sector are not providing "essential" services, in the sense that public health, safety, or security would be immediately threatened if their services were temporarily disrupted. Most public

41

employees are doing the same kind of work as is done by employees in the private sector, and equity would dictate that their union activity should be governed differently than it is in the private sector only if the inherent structure of the labour market is sufficiently different between the two sectors to justify it. But, there is no doubt that the relationship between governments as employers and their employees has a somewhat different character from employer-employee relations in the private sector, whether the government is municipal, provincial, or federal. There are a number of considerations which account for this difference.

THE ROLE OF THE MARKET IN CONSTRAINING UNION DEMANDS

One of the most important considerations is the influence of the market in the government sector, compared to the private sector. The market operates in the public sector, but far more effectively on the supply side than on the demand side. In the long run, the supply of labour to the public sector is a function of the price paid for labour by the public employer relative to what workers can earn elsewhere. This offers considerable assurance that public employees, with or without collective bargaining, will not for long be underpaid, at least at entry level jobs. The influence of the private sector in holding up public sector wage levels is virtually assured because most public employees work in urban areas, where there are a number of substitutable and competing private and public employers in the labour market.

However, in the private sector the discipline of the market not only helps to assure that employees are not paid too little by their employers, when compared to their earning opportunities elsewhere. The discipline of the market also serves to constrain the demands of employees for wage and fringe benefit increases, since they know that gains in compensation which exceed productivity gains must usually be paid for in terms of reduced employment. Market imposed unemployment is an important restraint on unions in the private sector. In the public sector, the trade-off between benefits won and employment seems much less important. The products of government are generally financed through taxes and provided to the population "free of charge." Hence, the individual taxpayer has no incentive to curtail his consumption of the government product when union gains have made it too expensive, in his view, because his actions alone will not suffice to reduce his tax burden. Only concerted action by the taxpayers could reduce public expense by curtailing government production and the employment that it requires. In most instances, this concerted action will not take place, not only because of the difficulty of organizing the taxpayers, but also because there are usually no close substitutes for the products and services provided by government, so that the demand for them is relatively inelastic. Because much government activity is a monopoly, product competition, non-union or otherwise, does not exert the downward pressure on costs and wages that it does in the private sector.[32]

Even if taxpayers should become sufficiently irate over their rising tax burden to demand curtailment of some government activity, there is no necessary link between the activity which is curtailed and the activity in which costs have risen. Thus, it may be gains won by teachers that threaten to require a tax increase, but taxpayer revolt may be averted by reducing expenditures on sports facilities and extra-curricular activities in schools rather than by dismissing some teachers and increasing class size. Or the tax increase that would otherwise be required because of gains won by clerical and office staff of the provincial public service might be avoided by curtailing expenditures made on maintenance of the grounds surrounding provincial public buildings. Even when the government decides that it must curtail the employment of the group which has negotiated a wage increase, it will typically find it far easier, politically, to do this by restricting new hirings rather than laying off current employees. Hence, the close relationship between increased economic benefits and unemployment

43

which exists in most of the private sector does not exist in the public sector, and therefore does not serve as a significant deterrent to the demands of public sector unions.

THE PUBLIC EMPLOYER'S WILL TO RESIST

There is a second, perhaps more important, consideration in accounting for the difference between public and private sector labour relations. Not only is there less market deterrent to the demands of public sector unions, compared to private sector unions; but, furthermore, the public employer has less incentive to resist the demands of his employees than does the private sector employer. The private sector employer is primarily interested in maximizing profits, and he, therefore, will resist union demands that exceed increases in productivity, for if he accepts such demands he will suffer a loss in profits. The public sector employer, too, is interested in keeping labour costs from rising too rapidly, for that is one measure of how well he is doing his job.

However, another measure of how well he is doing his job which is more visible to the public is the frequency and duration of disruptions in public services caused by the strike or slowdown activities of disgruntled employees. Since there is no good substitute for most public services, the public is acutely aware of, and often mightily inconvenienced by, any disruption in their provision. In the event of a public sector strike, there is usually immediate and vociferous pressure put on the government employer by the affected public to end it. By contrast, if the government employer takes the other route of avoiding a work stoppage by acceding to employee demands, the public is less likely to become aroused about this even if the eventual consequence is a rapid rise in the expense of government. This is because it is very difficult for the taxpayer to assess the effect that any settlement will have on his tax burden, since revenues come from a number of different tax sources as well as from intergovernmental transfers, and since some of the provisions of the settlement may not result in significant public costs until years later. In the absence of strong taxpayer involvement in public sector labour negotiations, the public employer may be too readily inclined to accede to employee demands, since this will yield him the multiple benefits of easing recruiting efforts, smoothing day-to-day operational conflicts and expanding the size of his empire, as measured by his total budget.

None of this is intended to deny that there can be periods of intense public dissatisfaction with some aspects of government, during which public antipathy to the demands of public employee unions is very strong. During such periods, the path of least resistance for the public employer may be to grant only minimal concessions to the union negotiating position, even if that should precipitate a strike. However, these periods, during which the will of the public employer to resist demands made by his employees is strong, are inevitably transitory, due to the tremendous costs involved in effectively organizing public opinion.

EMPIRICAL EVIDENCE

Empirical support for the arguments made here is available in the results of an econometric study made by Jean-Michel Cousineau and Robert Lacroix for the Economic Council of Canada. The variable of interest in this study is the percentage chage in base wage rates resulting from major collective agreements negotiated between 1967 and 1975. Explanatory equations for this variable are estimated separately for public and private sector bargaining units. The results indicate that the determinants of wage increases negotiated over this period are significantly different between public and private sectors. In particular, wage rates in the private sector were found to be twice as responsive to labour market conditions as wage rates in the public sector. Analysis of the size of the coefficients estimated for the public sector led Cousineau and Lacroix to conclude that "labour market conditions could not be considered a very significant factor in explaining wage developments in this sector."[33] In other words, in comparison to the private sector, wage increases won by bargaining units in the public sector are less constrained by employment opportunities in the economy. Presumably, this is because public sector employees are more confident that their wage increases will not result in unemployment for them, no matter what the state of the labour market might be for private sector employees.

CONSEQUENCES ARISING FROM PUBLIC/PRIVATE SECTOR PAY DIFFERENCES

The consequences which may result from this difference in labour market behaviour between the public and private sectors are serious. They may be divided into two major categories: macroeconomic and political. Cousineau and Lacroix explain one of the macroeconomic consequences as follows:

"[B]ecause wages in the public sector show a relative increase during a recession, the unemployed may prefer to continue seeking work rather than accept the wage conditions offered by employers in the private sector. This 'wait and see' attitude may be due to the fact that workers hope to find employment in the sector in which a relative increase in wages is anticipated or because they cannot appreciate real labour market conditions in an economy where numerous wage settlements are unresponsive to the real economic situation...

If some or all the unemployed continue to demand high wages, wages in the private sector will not be able to adjust sufficiently, jobs will not be created, and unemployment will remain above its 'natural' rate. Thus, rigidity of wages in the public sector causes wage rigidity in the economy as a whole and persistent unemployment. Obviously, the significance of this phenomenon will depend on the importance of the role played in the labour market as a whole by the public sector, where salaries are more rigid. In this sense, growth in the public sector might be correlated with the persistence of ever-increasing unemployment rates.''[34]

Further, the government's attempts to reduce resulting unemployment through monetary and fiscal expansion are likely to have inflationary consequences.
Finally,

"the considerably higher wages obtained by workers in the public sector [during a recession, with or without inflation] are a further source of industrial conflict in the private sector: unions demand comparable wage levels but [unlike the public employer] the particular firm must consider its ability to meet such demands.''[35]

With respect to the political consequences arising from public sector union activity, the end result is that public employee unions have what many consider to be excessive power to influence important public decisions. Employee groups, like all other interest groups in our society, have the opportunity to influence public decisions by lobbying activities with the appropriate government body. But, in addition to that, many public employee groups in Canada today have the unique and tremendous power to influence public decisions by threatening to withhold their services. In the private sector, the strike is an economic weapon; but in the public sector it is a political weapon. The public employer suffers no financial loss during a work stoppage. Tax revenues are collected, whether or not there are disruptions in service. But, partly for that reason, the political costs to the public employer of a work stoppage are often substantial. By capitalizing on these political costs, employee unions may increase their portion of the public budget; they may effectively raise the average quality of public service manpower by winning wages which are high relative to the private sector; they may change the manner in which some public services are provided; and they may influence a host of other issues, all of which, in a democratic society, should be decided jointly by the public affected. This is not to say that the employees are not a part of the public affected; of course, they are. But they are only a *part* of that public, and the full transplant of collective bargaining to the public sector may result in such disproportionate power for employee groups that the interests of the rest of the public are unprotected.

The following chapters discuss the policy alternatives which may be used in an attempt to balance the desire of public employees to exercise some control over their working conditions against the broader public interest. The first section considers the situation in which there is essentially no collective bargaining permitted to public employees. The second section considers the situation where collective bargaining is permitted but strikes are not, with all disputes resolved by compulsory arbitration. The third section considers the situation in which both bargaining and the strike are permitted to public employees. The fourth and final section contains our recommendations for modification of public sector labour relations.

CHAPTER SIX
Policy Alternatives

A. CONSULTATION

This is the model which applied in all jurisdictions in Canada (except Saskatchewan) prior to the policy liberalization of the middle to late 1960s. It is the model which still applies in the federal and most state public sectors in the United States. In this model, while public employees may be permitted to unionize and to attempt to influence their employer's decisions concerning wages, fringes, and working conditions, their efforts are limited to consultation and lobbying. Strikes are prohibited and no provision is made for arbitration, so that any differences between employer and employee groups are ultimately settled unilaterally by the employer's decision.

It was the dissatisfaction of public employees with this model which ultimately led to the legislative changes in the 1960s which introduced formal collective bargaining into all public sector jurisdictions in Canada. Two important factors causing employee dissatisfaction with the consultation model in the federal public service were:

1) the cynical attitude of the government, alluded to earlier, in which the consultative rights of public employee groups were regarded as nothing more than ritual, form with no substance; and

49

2) the readiness of the government, whenever expedient, to rely on wage restraint in the public sector as an easy target for cost-cutting, regardless of the dictates of the prevailing wage principle.

This model might have been considerably more tolerable had the government been more consistent in its application of the prevailing wage principle; i.e., in ensuring comparability between public and private sector employees. Public employees, quite understandably, felt unfairly used when their wages became one of the government's principal policy tools in combatting budgetary or inflationary pressures, especially when private sector wages continued to rise.

Added to that, as public sector employment expanded relative to private sector employment, it became increasingly more difficult to persuade those employed in the public sector that the privileges of government employment justified the loss of influence over their working conditions that they were accustomed to in private sector employment.[36]

Even if it were feasible, we would not recommend a return to this model for public sector labour relations in Canada, since we do not think that unilateral employer control would foster either labour peace or the public interest.

B. COMPULSORY ARBITRATION

This is the model which covers all public employees in several of the provinces currently. Under this model, public employees may bargain over most issues, including wages, but any impasse in negotiations must be resolved by compulsory arbitration. The strike is prohibited.

Currently, all jurisdictions prohibit strikes by both public and private employees in almost all instances of disputes over rights—that is, over the terms of an existing contract. Such disputes are resolved by arbitration. If there is to be collective bargaining coupled with a strike prohibition, then it becomes necessary that all disputes—both rights and interest—be resolved by some form of arbitration. One of the arguments often raised in opposition to the compulsory arbitration model is that arbitration of interest disputes is unsuitable, because arbitration is designed to adjudicate disputes over the interpretation of agreements, where the existing collective agreement provides a firm foundation for the arbitrator's decision. In the case of interest disputes, however, there is no existing collective agreement and the arbitrator has the far more difficult task of determining what a "reasonable" and "acceptable" collective agreement should look like.

While there is considerable merit to this argument with respect to non-wage disputes, it is far less valid when applied to public sector compensation disputes. This is because the generally accepted principle of parity or comparability with the private sector serves to give the public sector arbitrator some firm criteria on which to base his judgement in interest disputes over compensation, much as the collective agreement does for rights disputes. In fact, if bargaining over compensation is to be permitted at all in the public sector, acceptance of the prevailing wage principle makes arbitration rather than the strike the logical means by which to resolve an impasse in wage negotiations. If both sides agree, in principle, that the terms of the settlement should reflect conditions for comparable workers in the private sector, then any wage dispute between employer and employee negotiators must reduce to the factual issue of establishing comparability. This is the kind of issue at which arbitration functions best. The problems with the comparability principle currently being experienced in the federal sector, relating to the determination of the appropriate universe for comparison and of the appropriate wage offset for non-wage differences between the public and private sectors, are not intractable. By relying on disequilibrium signals—shortages or queues for public service job vacancies—public sector arbitrators can permit the market to tell them whether existing compensation packages in the public sector are comparable to those in the private sector.[37] By contrast, resort to the strike to resolve public sector wage disputes effectively dispenses with the comparability criterion, as unions simply wield whatever power they have to extract the largest feasible settlement.

Problems with arbitration

However, there are good arguments raised against the wholesale substitution of compulsory arbitration for the right to strike in the public sector. One of the most important of these arguments is based on the "chilling effect" that arbitration apparently has on negotiations. The reason for the chilling effect is easy enough to understand. If either the public employer or the union reckons that a third party award will be more advantageous than a negotiated settlement, that party will employ tactics to ensure an impasse in negotiations so that the dispute will be submitted to the third party for resolution. This is a problem which is impossible to solve completely in a system of compulsory arbitration. It is often suggested, however, that the chilling effect can be reduced by fashioning a system of post-impasse procedures sufficiently diverse and uncertain as to foreclose the possibility of either side being able to calculate with any accuracy that it would receive advantageous treatment by the third party.

Even if simple arbitration is the only procedure specified by legislation in the event of an impasse, considerable uncertainty about the outcome of arbitration can be maintained by allowing each party to select one member, from whatever source, of a three person arbitration panel, with the chairman (the third person) selected by mutual agreement between the two panel members selected by the disputants.

Some authorities have suggested that a device to further reduce the chilling effect is "final offer" arbitration, in which the arbitrator's choice would be limited to either the employer's final position or the union's final position—all of one or the other. It is believed that the onus thus placed on each party to arrive at a position more reasonable and acceptable than his adversary's will result in the positions of the parties actually meeting on some middle ground, thus eliminating the need to resort to arbitration at all, or, failing that, substantially reducing the areas of disagreement that must be resolved by arbitration.

In those situations involving essential services, where any strike is intolerable, some form of arbitration must be used if there is to be any collective bargaining for these employees. In these instances, the final offer variant may have considerable merit if it reduces the likelihood that the negotiations will stall. However, in the public sector, as in the private sector, we must consider whether the third party costs that will arise because of a strike in "non-essential" services are large enough to justify the substitution of compulsory arbitration with its own set of associated costs. The major hope for employer-employee harmony is not the post-impasse procedure, but the bargaining process; not the resolution of impasses, but their avoidance. No matter what gimmicks are added to the arbitration process, much of its chilling effect on negotiations will remain.[38] Hence, if compulsory arbitration is specified as the only acceptable post-impasse procedure, the need to resort to it is likely to occur quite frequently. But, as already mentioned, apart from disputes over public sector compensation levels, the arbitrator has no clear guidelines on which to base his judgements. Hence, he may have great difficulty in persuading one or both sides of the justice of his decisions, especially when they concern work rules or standards. At present, with the lack of appropriate labour market disequilibrium data for guidance, and with the use of lawyers as arbitrators rather than economists who are trained to interpret the economic data, even the justice of decisions over compensation levels is difficult to defend. The result is that an often unpopular settlement is imposed on both parties, who must live with it with more or less good grace. Past experience indicates, however, that dissatisfaction with an imposed settlement will surface in one way or another.

On the employees' side, it may take the form of absenteeism, work slowdowns, increased grievance claims, and even illegal strikes. In fact, empirical studies in the United States seem to show that anti-strike laws and interest arbitration have little impact on the incidence of strikes.[39] While the imposition of severe sanctions against employees engaging in illegal strikes may help to reduce their incidence, it is neither desirable nor feasible to impose sanctions against public employees *en masse*. In those jurisdictions where public employees have become convinced that strike prohibition is unfair to them, strikes are likely to occur no matter what legislation exists. Where this happens, policy may have little choice but to accept the strike while seeking to reduce its effects. Consequently, the next section considers a model in which the strike is legal.

C. BARGAINING WITH THE STRIKE

This is the route chosen by the federal jurisdiction and many of the provinces since the 1960s. In this model, bargaining, even over compensation levels, is permitted, and the strike is legal for all but essential employees.

If strikes in the public sector which do not create a true emergency are to be permitted without interference, and if bargaining is to include the level of employee compensation, it becomes important that the public employer design his operations so as to minimize the extent to which his employees can win excessive demands by exploiting the lack of close substitutes for most government services.

Approaches to reduce the vulnerability of the public employer

Because of the lack of close substitutes, most strikes in the public sector inconvenience people, and these people are voters. Because the costs of settlement may frequently be passed on to other political units or be hidden in the bowels of an incomprehensible public budget,

> "voters will tend to choose political leaders who avoid inconveniencing strikes over those who work to minimize the costs of settlements at the price of a strike. . . . The net

54

effect is that the typical... political structure is altogether too vulnerable to strikes by public employees, and other groups in the political process are thereby disadvantaged."[40]

A few suggestions are offered below which aim to reduce the vulnerability of the public employer.

1) Contingency planning

There are three types of approaches which can be used in combination to reduce the vulnerability of the public employer to strikes. The first approach seeks to lessen the impact of the strike itself, by taking advance measures to minimize the inconvenience to the public that a work stoppage would cause. This approach includes the obvious measure of contingency planning for substitutes or alternatives to the usual manner of provision of services, if at all possible. At a minimum, a sufficient number of employees should be designated to maintain the provision of essential services. Further, the public employer should insist on limiting any union security clauses to the "Rand formula" or agency shop, in which all employees in the bargaining unit may be required to pay a "bargaining fee" to the union, but are not required to become union members. In this case, those non-union employees who do not support the strike may continue to report for work without fear of fines or loss of employment arising from union imposed sanctions against them.

In the longer run, the inconvenience that an employee strike can impose on the public can be reduced by automating the employees' most critical functions, or by contracting out for at least a portion of them. To the extent that this is not feasible, some experts in the area have suggested that injured third parties to public sector strikes should have some recourse in the law to demand compensation from government and striking labour for the breaking of the implicit "social contract" of the continuous provision of the public services.[41]

2) Work force adjustments

This points up the importance of the second type of approach which can reduce the vulnerability of the public employer to strikes. The second approach seeks to constrain the demands of public employees by impressing upon them that, even in the public sector where the demand for the ultimate service produced is fairly inelastic, excessive gains in compensation can be made to result in reduced employment. Public employment can be cut directly when public employees become too expensive, either by automating their functions or contracting them out to companies in the private sector. When advantageous, the public employer should be free to accomplish this cut in public employment by layoffs, rather than having to rely on attrition alone. If their employees are going to exercise full collective bargaining rights, it is important that public employers not be hampered in their response by concern for other public goals that would not be imposed on private sector employers. In particular, it is important that public employers retain the right to exercise their judgement concerning the size of their work force, the introduction of new technology, and contracting out, since this is the only significant way in which market constraints may operate on public sector unions. Neither the collective agreement nor labour legislation should curtail the prerogatives of the public employer in this area.

An additional device that public employers can on occasion use to advantage in constraining the demands of their employee unions is the lockout. Currently, in all jurisdictions except British Columbia, the public employer is forbidden by legislation to employ the lockout against his employees. This has permitted post office employees, for example, to disrupt postal services for lengthy periods by rotating strikes without serious financial penalty to any employee. Pressure on the employees to settle, or to continue to negotiate without disruption, could be greatly increased if rotating strikes resulted in a lockout of all employees by the employer. Further, the public employer should be free to impose short-run layoffs on other workers idled because of the strike, or to employ replacements for the striking employees. It is detrimental to the public interest, and to the cause of employer-employee harmony, to give public employees the rights enjoyed by unions in the private sector while refusing to the public employer the powers enjoyed by his counterpart in the private sector.

3) Public relations

The third type of approach which can reduce the vulnerability of the public employer to strikes would seek to decrease public willingness to call for settlements without sufficient regard for the costs involved. "Any measure that sharpens the public's awareness of the costs of a settlement...will tend to decrease the political pressure for a precipitous settlement."[42] There are numerous ways in which the public's awareness of the implications of the settlement may be increased; which way will be effective in any specific case will depend on the particular level of government and the type of employee involved. Publication of the proposed salary levels, by type of job performed, is one device.

> "Where these salaries seem higher than those received for comparable work in the private sector, public sympathy for the strikers will not be very great, and political leaders may be less fearful of a backlash at the polls because they resist union demands at the price of a strike."[43]

> "Another device might be to specify in tax bills the allocation of taxes among various functions of government or the amount attributable to collective agreements. Taxpayer groups...may thus be aided in leading opposition against union demands."[44]

At least at the local level, settlements reached might be subject to approval by a referendum among registered voters. The referendum, in effect, asks the voters to approve the estimated tax consequences of the settlement.

57

"The referendum device increases the visibility of a settlement's costs and places it on those voters with the most power to resist. Furthermore, union leaders are encouraged to make their deal with elected officials rather than risk the unknowns of a referendum. Such settlements are apt to be smaller than those that would follow strikes under present structures. The officials, moreover, have an incentive to settle and thereby claim credit for avoiding a strike, but are able. . .to escape the dilemma of choosing between the wrath of those inconvenienced by a strike and those enraged by increased taxes."[45]

Prospects for success

Despite our discussion of ways in which we think the public interest might be better protected within the context of a non-emergency strike model, we do not recommend the continuation or further extension of this model as it currently exists in Canada. The principal considerations which account for our position have already been discussed in earlier sections. The major distinguishing characteristic of public sector employment, as opposed to private sector employment, is the absence of market constraints on public employee demands for higher compensation. The prevailing wage principle is founded on the equity and the efficiency of maintaining comparability between public and private sector compensation levels. There is apparently wide public acceptance of its justice. When public employees may bargain and strike over compensation, the principle of comparability with the private sector is effectively replaced by the principle of more pay to those with more power. The approaches outlined in this section to reduce the vulnerability of the public sector employer to strike demands are all measures designed to reduce the power of public employee groups. Many of the measures proposed are feeble, at best. They may be effective if used forcefully by the public employer, but, as we indicated earlier, in many instances the public employer has little incentive to do so, since there are some benefits and few costs to him by simply acquiescing to employee demands.

Consequently, we are not optimistic that the public interest can be adequately protected in a model which permits bargaining and strikes over compensation to public employees. Because of the acquiescence of the public employer, even bargaining in the arbitration model may not adequately protect the public interest. We would much prefer to eliminate what we view as the fundamental problem, characteristic of all jurisdictions in Canada at present, of permitting public sector employees to bargain at all over compensation levels. This is the focus of the next section.

D. LIMITED BARGAINING

If we could newly fashion public sector labour policy, we would advocate a system of limited collective bargaining in which overall compensation levels were not negotiable, although the division between pay and fringe benefits might be a legitimate topic for bargaining. The overall level of compensation for each job type would be determined in each jurisdiction by an independent and continuing wage board, whose decisions would be based on strict private sector comparability guidelines.[46] The accurate determination of comparability would be based on a comparison of average wage and fringe benefit levels between the public and private sectors, supplemented by labour market disequilibrium signals, where the existence of vacancies which are difficult to fill with the usual quality workers would indicate the need to increase compensation in that job classification, while a queue of qualified applicants would indicate that compensation was too high. Both employer and employee groups would be welcome to make submissions to the wage board, but bargaining as such would not take place. Since the level of compensation would not be subject to collective bargaining, naturally, strikes to win increased compensation would be prohibited.

Issues other than the level of compensation would, as now,

be subject to collective bargaining. These might include the division of compensation increases between pay and fringe benefits, as well as work rules, disciplinary, and grievance procedures. Further, as indicated earlier, some of the current restrictions on bargaining in the public sector on non-wage issues could be relaxed by the introduction of what we have called two-tier bargaining, so that bargaining over hiring, promotion, and classification standards might be possible as well. This requires further study. However, existing prohibitions on collective bargaining over issues which have important implications for public policy, such as decentralization of the governance of schools or the creation of a civilian board to review police conduct, would remain. On such issues, employees have, and should have, only the right to lobby in competition with other groups with equally legitimate interests.

For most workers, an impasse in negotiations on non-wage issues could be met either by the strike or by voluntary submission of the dispute to binding arbitration, although the arbitration route would require the consent of both sides to the dispute. However, in certain bargaining units, some employees may be designated as essential, so that any legal strike would be limited; in this instance, the employee group could seek binding arbitration even without the consent of the employer. This serves as a counterbalance to the employer's ability to eliminate the strike as a viable weapon for some bargaining units by designating a large proportion of the unit as essential.

Amnesty in the event of illegal strike activity would not be available through the collective bargaining route. To ensure this, the responsibility for prosecution of illegal strike activity (either by employee or employer) would rest with a public prosecutor who would be empowered to initiate prosecution whether or not charges were pressed by the adversaries.

Merits of this model

The merits we find in this model are implicit in our discussion of the previous three models. We think that the concept of bargaining over the level of public sector compensation is inconsistent with the principle of the prevailing wage. It is widely seen as just that public sector employees receive no more and no less in total compensation than comparable employees in the private sector. Given that view, it is not unjust to public employees to set their compensation levels by a wage board, rather than by bargaining, so long as the wage board is competent to establish comparability and is independent of government pressures to modify their considered decision in response to other government policy needs. The wage board we propose is very similar to the Industrial Peace Commission suggested by Leland Hazard, of the Carnegie Institute of Technology, except that we think it essential that the board have the authority to *set* wages, rather than simply to make recommendations as Hazard suggests. In order to free the commission or board from political influence, Hazard suggests that its members, who would be drawn from labour, industry, the professions, and the universities, be appointed on a long-term basis much as Supreme Court judges are.[47] In this way, governments would be prevented from pressuring the board into decisions which allow the government to revert to past practice of using public sector pay rates as a macroeconomic policy tool. The substitution of an independent wage board for bargaining over compensation in the public sector not only protects the taxpayer from excessive gains by public employees; it also protects public employees from inappropriate measures taken against them by the government during periods of belt-tightening. For these reasons, we do not think it totally unrealistic to propose, as we do here, that one of the bargaining rights already exercised by public employees in all jurisdictions in Canada be withdrawn.

Our recommendation that the strike be available to public employees in the event of an impasse in negotiations over all bargainable non-wage issues represents an extension of rights not yet exercised by some provincial public employees. As indicated in our discussion of the compulsory arbitration

61

model, there is no reliable criterion by which interest disputes over non-wage issues, even in the public sector, may be resolved by an arbitrator. Hence, the only solution to such disputes which is likely to be accepted by both sides as fair is one which they hammer out between themselves via negotiations and, if necessary, the strike. As in the private sector, conciliation should be available to the disputants if they request it. Further, the right to voluntarily submit their disputes to binding arbitration should help to reduce the incidence of disruptions in the public sector even though the right to strike remains. The major factor which should reduce the current level of work stoppages in the public sector, however, is the elimination of bargaining over compensation.

Our recommendation that amnesty for illegal strike activity not be subject to bargaining seems an essential element to the preservation of any system of labour relations. If labour legislation is going to specify that certain activities are prohibited, then sanctions must necessarily be taken against offenders in order to make the prohibition meaningful. If those engaged in an illegal strike may escape sanctions through bargaining, then we risk the deterioration of the labour relations system into labour anarchy.

CHAPTER SEVEN
Conclusion

In the preceding sections, we have argued that market constraints, operating through profits and unemployment, are absent in the public sector. Since the tradition of job security is strong in the public sector, there is little effective deterrent to prevent public employees from using their collective bargaining privileges to demand very large wage increases. Unlike employees in the private sector, public sector employees need rarely fear that excessive wage gains will cause their unemployment by forcing their employer to curtail or close operations, since the government has no profit constraint. It can use its power to tax, to borrow, or (in the case of the federal government) to print money to pay the increased costs of operation. Each of these fiscal operations may have some direct inflationary consequences for the economy.

Further, large wage gains by public sector employees may have undesirable consequences in the private sector, in the form of unemployment and labour unrest. These can occur because private sector employees may resist accepting wages lower than the wages being paid comparable employees in the public sector. Hence, private sector unions may become more militant in their wage demands, in an attempt to catch up to the public sector. Because private sector employers do face profit constraints, they may be unable to grant wage increases as large as those obtained by public sector workers, and numerous work stoppages may result. To the extent that private sector employers do not match the wages obtained in the public sector, unemployment may increase, as members of the labour force "hold out" for one of the more lucrative jobs in the public sector.[48]

The end result is that unfettered collective bargaining in the public sector can have undesirable consequences for economic stability. Economic stability could be better maintained if public sector wages were set according to prevailing wages in the private sector, where market constraints are available to rationalize the wage levels set. Indeed, in a number of recent statements, the federal government has reaffirmed its intention to rely on the principle of the prevailing wage in future negotiations with its employees.

We would go further. We believe that it is fundamentally inconsistent to engage in collective bargaining over wages, while advocating strict adherence to the prevailing wage principle. Inevitably, in a bargaining situation, the employees' union will seek the highest wage settlement obtainable regardless of the comparability criterion. Consequently, employees in bargaining units with little bargaining power might acquiesce to the government's position and accept comparability with private sector employees; but employees in bargaining units with great bargaining power (i.e., those who can impose serious costs on the government or the public by withholding their services) may well insist on more.

ELIMINATION OF BARGAINING OVER COMPENSATION IN THE PUBLIC SECTOR

We would recommend that bargaining over pay be eliminated in the public sector. We would advocate a system of limited collective bargaining in which overall compensation levels are not negotiable, although the division between pay and fringe benefits might be a legitimate topic for bargaining. The overall level of compensation for each job type would be determined in each jurisdiction by an independent and continuing wage board, whose decisions would be based on strict private sector comparability guidelines. Both employer and employee groups would be welcome to make submissions to the wage board, but bargaining as such would not take place. Since the level of compensation would not be subject to collective bargaining, naturally, strikes to win increased compensation would be prohibited. Issues other than the level of compensation would, as now, be subject to collective bargaining. If public sector compensation levels are set by a wage board, rather than being subject to collective bargaining and the strike, this should go far toward reducing the incidence of work stoppages in the public sector even though strikes may still occur if bargaining over non-wage issues breaks down.

CONTINUANCE OF BARGAINING OVER NON-WAGE ISSUES

Many people would go further, and advocate the total prohibition of strikes in the public sector, maintaining that any service important enough to be provided publicly is important enough to be provided without disruption. If strikes are prohibited in the public sector, then binding arbitration must be substituted as the means by which an impasse in negotiations over non-wage issues is resolved. In this case, we would favour the "final-offer" variety of arbitration, in which the chilling effect of arbitration on negotiations is minimized. However, we suspect that a total strike prohibition is simply not a feasible option in the Canadian public sector of today.

Public employees have demonstrated that they are willing to strike, illegally if necessary, when they are convinced that they are not being treated fairly. Even without a strike, employee discontent can take the form of more subtle job actions (or inaction) which can be just as disruptive as a strike. While the substitution of binding arbitration for the strike as the means by which bargaining impasses are resolved in the public sector is currently a popular idea, those experienced with it are negative to the idea. This is because, although arbitration is very useful in resolving disputes concerning the interpretation of an existing contract where the language of the contract provides the arbitrator a firm foundation for his judgements, it founders when the arbitrator must fashion a new contract out of the arguments of the employer and the union. There seems to be no reliable criterion by which interest disputes over non-wage issues in the public sector may be resolved by an arbitrator. Hence, at present, the only solution to such disputes which is likely to be accepted by both sides as fair is one which they hammer out between themselves, via negotiations and, if necessary, the strike.

LEGISLATIVE SAFEGUARDS

If the strike is not to be prohibited in the public sector though, it is important that the public employer not be hamstrung in his bargaining efforts. In particular, he should not be prohibited from employing the lockout if that would enhance his bargaining position. Further, he should not be prohibited from laying off other employees who are idled because of a work stoppage, or from contracting out to the private sector whenever that is a feasible and less costly way of providing service. Further, there should be standing legislation in all jurisdictions which provides a mechanism for assuring the continuation of essential services in the event of a work stoppage, and for terminating the work stoppage altogether if it threatens the health or safety of the population. Finally, amnesty in the event of illegal strike activity should not be available through the collective bargaining route. To ensure this, the responsibility for prosecution of illegal strike activity (either by employee or employer) should rest with a public prosecutor who would be empowered to initiate prosecution whether or not charges were pressed by the adversaries. This ensures that some deterrent against illegal activity will exist and, hence, provides some protection for third parties in the general public who are often seriously injured by disruptions in public services. Otherwise, their only alternative would be private damage suits against the offender, but this is unlikely to be a very effective alternative because of the legal costs involved if suits are filed individually, and the organizational costs involved if a class action suit is filed.

REITERATION

The fundamental point made here is that the maintenance of public/private sector pay parity is inconsistent with public sector pay bargaining. The maintenance of parity is important for reasons of equity, efficiency, and macroeconomic stability. The introduction of pay bargaining in the public sector replaces the parity principle with the principle of more pay to those with more power, and this virtually assures the appearance of a pay premium to public sector employees. Under present institutional arrangements, there is no effective way for the public to influence public sector settlements on an on-going basis, so as to achieve and maintain parity with the private sector. The independent pay-setting board suggested here is intended to create an institutional arrangement whereby the public interest in public/private pay parity could be better served than it is at present.

PROBLEMS IN IMPLEMENTATION

There would, of course, be problems in implementing this proposal. One set of problems is operational, concerning the appropriate definition of "comparability with the private sector." The second set of problems is political, concerning the feasibility of withdrawing the right to bargain over pay from public sector employees. While it must be recognized that these problems are serious, they may, nevertheless, be amenable to resolution.

1) Operational problems

There are two aspects to the operational problem of defining comparability: 1) determination of a set of comparable private sector workers to use as a reference group for each category of public sector employees; and 2) monetary evaluation of their "full" pay, including working conditions and fringe benefits as well as wages or salaries. In the absence of market information, any pay board decision concerning the set of private sector employees to be used as the reference or comparison group, or the monetary value to be placed on certain non-wage aspects of employment, is certain to be viewed as arbitrary and unjust by at least some of the parties affected. But these decisions need not and should not be made in the absence of market information. Indeed, reliance on labour market disequilibrium signals can obviate the need for detailed consideration of such matters. If public sector "full" pay is too low relative to the private sector, it will become difficult to fill public sector vacancies without a significant lowering of the qualifications usually considered necessary for the job. If public sector "full" pay is high relative to the private sector, there will be queues of qualified applicants clamoring for public sector jobs. Thus, the actions of employees and job seekers in the market will inform the pay board as to whether current public sector pay scales are competitive with private sector pay scales for comparable workers.[49]

2) Political problems

The political feasibility of withdrawing a bargaining privilege now universally available to public sector employees in Canada is the more serious problem. Public interest arguments clearly favour this withdrawal, but to achieve its peaceful implementation it would be helpful to persuade public sector employees that it is in their personal interests as well. Arguments can be made to this effect, particularly in the current climate of public antipathy to the public sector and its alleged excesses. Although market forces make it impossible for the public employer to retain his labour force for long if pay scales are not competitive with the private sector, "exploitation" of this sort may succeed in the short run. Thus, during the recent experience with wage-price controls in Canada, evidence indicates that the government was more successful in holding down public sector pay increases than private sector increases.[50] Going further back in our history, there is evidence that whenever governments are forced to economize, one target is public service pay scales regardless of the dictates of private sector comparability.[51] The substitution of an independent wage board for bargaining over pay in the public sector would not only protect the taxpayer from excessive gains by public employees; it would also protect public employees from inappropriate measures taken against them by the government during periods of public sector belt-tightening. The wage board would ensure that public sector employees do as well as they could expect to do in the private sector, whatever the current attitude toward government activity. In periods like the present, where there is widespread sentiment that public expenditures should be reduced as a proportion of our total national income, the operation of the public sector wage board would ensure that that result, if achieved, would be accomplished by a curtailment of government activity, rather than by a punitive pay policy toward public sector employees. Pay comparability between public and private sector workers would be maintained. This is the outcome of an efficiently operating labour market, and the operation of the wage board would assure this outcome for public sector employees without the need for them to incur the financial costs of a strike to obtain it.

TABLE 1
Union Membership as a Percentage of Employees by Industry

Year	Forestry	Mining	Manufac- turing	Construc- tion	Transportation, Communications & Public Utilities	Trade	Finance	Services	Public Adminis- tration	All Indus- tries
1962	44.9	50.1	42.7	48.2	56.6	5.4	.2	8.8	23.3	28.9
1963	55.3	42.5	41.6	46.3	55.2	5.2	.2	8.7	24.1	28.4
1964	48.3	48.8	42.7	47.6	55.1	5.8	.3	9.3	25.4	27.9
1965	56.2	48.7	43.0	46.0	53.6	6.0	.3	9.6	25.2	28.2
1966	63.0	51.1	44.0	48.3	53.5	6.4	.2	10.1	39.2	29.3
1967	63.5	50.0	45.3	56.2	53.6	7.2	.2	10.4	53.8	31.5
1968	67.3	50.2	46.4	59.9	55.4	7.6	.2	11.6	54.8	32.2
1969	61.9	50.7	45.7	58.7	53.8	7.3	.6	12.1	60.0	32.0
1970	60.8	45.1	46.8	62.3	53.9	8.0	.5	12.7	75.7	33.0
1976	57.4	44.2	48.9	66.9	56.5	9.4	2.1	32.0	72.0	38.0

Note: The Agriculture, Fishing and Trapping divisions have been omitted because unionization was negligible throughout the period.

Sources: Employment figures were obtained from *Estimates of Employees by Province and Industry, 1961-1976*, Statistics Canada 72-516, Table 2, p. 13.

Union membership figures for 1962-1970 were obtained from *Union Growth in Canada in the Sixties*, Labour Canada, Table 1, pp. 16-17. For 1976 they were obtained from *Labour Gazette*, December 1977, pp. 562-563.

Although later data are available from CALURA reports, we have not presented them here because there is substantial underreporting of membership figures using CALURA figures alone.

TABLE 2
Percentage of Employees Covered by Collective Agreement
by Industry
1977

Industry	Office Employees	Non-Office Employees
Mining	12	84
Manufacturing	10	78
Transportation, Communications & Utilities	43	88
Trade	4	27
Finance	2	12
Services	29	48
Public Administration	89	94
All Industries	36	73

Note: The number of employees covered by a collective agreement overestimates the number of union members.

Source: Working Conditions in Canadian Industry, 1977, Economics and Research Branch, Labour Canada, Tables A and B, pp. 4-7.

TABLE 3.a
Work Stoppages in the Public Sector
(Public Administration, Health, Education, and Welfare)

Period	Number of stoppages	% *	Number of workers involved	% *	Man-days lost in these sectors	% *
1960-64	43	2.8	8,600	2.1	61,910†	1.0
1965-69	139	4.9	196,358	14.4	1,401,000	5.8
1970-74	345	9.5	604,953	28.2	3,393,390	10.5

* percentage of the whole economy
† corrected
Source: Andre Beaucage, *An Outline of the Canadian Labour Relations System,* Labour Canada, Employment Relations Branch, 1976, p. 38. Postal workers and employees of Crown corporations are not included in the public sector figures here.

TABLE 3.b
Work Stoppages in the Public Sector
(Public Administration, Health, Education, Welfare, and Communications)

Period	Number of stoppages	% *	Number of workers involved	% *	Man-days lost in these sectors	% *
1960-64	46	2.9	8,706	2.2	54,030	1.0
1965-69	161	5.7	245,058	17.9	2,101,650	8.6
1970-74	427	11.7	685,110	32.1	4,152,210	12.9

* percentage of the whole economy
Source: Strikes and Lockouts in Canada, Table 4, Economics and Research Branch, Labour Canada, various years.

TABLE 4.a
Work Stoppages Per Employee
Public Sector as a Percentage of the Whole Economy

Period	Number of stoppages	Number of workers involved	Man-days lost
1960-64	13.3	9.9	4.7
1965-69	22.2	65.3	26.3
1970-74	40.7	120.7	44.9

Sources: Table 3.a and *Estimates of Employees by Province and Industry, 1961-76,* Statistics Canada 72-516, Table 2, p. 13.

TABLE 4.b
Work Stoppages Per Unionized Employee
Public Sector as a Percentage of the Whole Economy

Period	Number of stoppages	Number of workers involved	Man-days lost
1960-64	29.5	22.1	10.5
1965-69	30.6	90.0	36.3
1970-74	31.7	94.0	35.0

Sources: Tables 3.a; *Union Growth in Canada in the Sixties,* Labour Canada, Table 1, pp. 16-17; and *Labour Gazette,* December 1977, p. 563.

TABLE 5
Annual Percentage Base Rate Wage Increases[1]

			Components within the Public Sector				
Year	*Private*	*Public*	*Federal*	*Provin-cial*	*Local*	*HEW*[2]	*Utilities*[3]
1976	9.4	11.1	11.5	11.3	10.6	10.7	12.3
1975	14.4	18.6	14.3	20.0	17.8	21.3	17.2
1974	14.4	14.8	11.3	15.1	12.6	17.8	18.0
1973	10.1	10.6	12.3	10.1	9.9	10.2	10.4
1972	9.2	7.2	8.9	8.0	7.6	6.5	7.9
1971	8.0	7.6	6.6	7.9	9.4	8.4	6.7
1970	8.6	8.4	8.4	7.2	9.9	8.9	7.7
1969	8.6	7.2	6.3	8.5	11.4	6.9	7.2
1968	8.1	7.6	7.0	8.3	7.0	10.0	6.5
1967	7.8	9.6	n/a	8.5	12.5	9.4	7.7
Average	9.9	10.3	9.6	10.5	10.9	11.0	10.2

Notes:
[1]From collective agreements covering 500 or more employees.
[2]Health, education, and welfare.
[3]Telephone, electrical, and water utilities.

Source: Morley Gunderson, ''Public-Private Wage and Non-Wage Differentials: Calculations from Published Tabulations,'' Institute for Research on Public Policy, 1977, p. 9.

TABLE 6
Ratio of Public to Business Sector Earnings

Year	Institu- tional[1]	Teachers /Profs.	Federal	Provin- cial	Muni- cipal	All Govt.[2]	All Public[3]
1975	.89	1.30	1.16	1.14	1.11	1.14	1.09
1974	.86	1.35	1.18	1.14	1.10	1.14	1.09
1973	.84	1.34	1.19	1.14	1.10	1.14	1.09
1972	.84	1.33	1.20	1.14	1.11	1.15	1.09
1971	.83	1.30	1.19	1.11	1.09	1.13	1.08
1970	.84	1.33	1.25	1.15	1.12	1.17	1.10
1969	.79	1.27	1.24	1.11	1.10	1.15	1.12
1968	.77	1.24	1.16	1.10	1.08	1.11	1.04
1967	.76	1.20	1.12	1.07	1.07	1.08	1.02
1966	.75	1.16	1.13	1.06	1.05	1.08	1.01
1965	.74	1.13	1.08	1.04	1.04	1.05	.98
1964	.74	1.11	1.07	1.01	1.04	1.04	.98
1963	.71	1.11	1.10	1.02	1.05	1.06	.99
1962	.70	1.09	1.05	1.01	1.04	1.04	.97
1961	.71	1.09	1.06	.99	1.03	1.03	.97
1960	.70	1.09	1.02	.97	1.04	1.01	.96
1959	.67	1.04	1.01	.97	1.04	1.00	.95
1958	.68	1.03	1.01	.97	1.02	1.00	.95
1957	.69	1.00	.99	.97	1.00	.99	.94
1956	.70	1.00	.98	.96	1.00	.98	.93
1955	.69	1.01	.99	.97	1.01	.99	.94
1954	.71	1.00	1.01	.96	1.03	1.00	.95
1953	.70	.99	.96	.96	1.01	.97	.93
1952	.71	.98	.99	.96	1.02	.99	.95
1951	.72	.97	.99	.96	1.02	.99	.95
1950	.75	.97	.96	.96	1.00	.97	.94
1949	.76	.97	.99	.96	1.01	.99	.95
1948	.74	.96	.98	.96	1.01	.98	.94
1947	.76	.95	.97	.99	1.00	.98	.94
1946	.78	.96	.97	.98	1.01	.98	.95

Notes:

[1]Mainly hospitals and non-profit organizations.

[2]Weighted average of federal, provincial, and municipal.

[3]Weighted average of federal, provincial, municipal, teachers/professors, and employees in institutions.

Source: Morley Gunderson, ''Public-Private Wage and Non-Wage Differentials: Calculations from Published Tabulations,'' Institute for Research on Public Policy, 1977, p. 2.

TABLE 7
Ratio of Municipal/Private Average Wages of Labourers, Various Communities, 1952-1973

Municipality	1952	1953	1954	1955	1956	1957	1958	1959	1960	19
Halifax	1.04	1.13	1.14	1.12	0.99	0.98	1.00	0.93	1.04	1.
Sydney	0.85	0.80	0.82	0.85	0.88	0.90	0.92	1.04	0.99	1.
Saint John	1.25	1.18	1.18	1.14	1.12	1.17	1.14	1.12	1.06	1.
Cap-Madeleine	0.66	0.60	0.62	0.62	0.60	n/a	0.63	0.73	0.74	0.
Hull	0.75	0.85	0.78	0.77	0.73	0.68	0.73	0.70	0.81	0.
Montreal	0.99	0.88	0.98	0.97	1.00	0.94	1.01	n/a	1.09	1.
Quebec	0.71	0.86	0.94	0.86	0.83	0.86	0.76	0.81	0.85	0.
Shawinigan	0.74	0.70	0.84	0.83	0.79	0.75	0.88	0.91	1.08	1.
Sherbrooke	1.09	1.12	1.10	1.07	1.08	0.96	1.06	1.08	1.23	1.
Trois-Rivieres	0.71	n/a	0.70	0.78	0.70	0.73	0.73	0.90	0.91	1.
Brantford	1.04	0.97	0.99	1.06	0.82	1.06	1.05	1.13	1.12	1.
Cambridge	0.88	0.97	0.93	0.93	0.83	0.96	1.04	1.08	0.97	1.
Chatham	1.13	1.15	1.00	0.84	0.84	0.84	0.88	0.93	1.01	0.
Cornwall	0.83	0.77	0.73	0.76	0.86	0.86	0.86	0.91	0.92	0.
Guelph	0.96	0.96	0.95	0.99	0.90	0.84	0.96	1.08	1.05	1.
Hamilton	0.83	n/a	0.94	0.93	0.84	0.89	0.91	0.94	0.96	0.
Kitchener	0.97	0.93	0.94	1.00	0.96	1.01	1.08	1.12	1.08	1.
London	0.91	0.90	0.98	0.99	1.02	0.98	1.03	n.a.	1.13	1.
Niagara Falls	0.82	0.90	n/a	1.00	0.98	0.96	0.97	0.90	1.02	1.
Oshawa	0.93	0.93	1.01	1.01	0.92	0.92	0.94	0.93	0.93	0.
Ottawa	0.92	1.03	1.06	1.16	1.07	1.02	1.25	1.16	1.15	1.
Peterborough	0.87	0.95	1.01	1.01	0.98	1.05	1.07	1.07	1.07	1.
St. Catharines	0.98	0.95	0.85	0.87	0.92	0.95	0.96	1.02	1.02	0.
Sarnia	0.89	0.96	0.95	0.98	0.96	0.95	0.97	0.98	0.96	0.
Sault Ste. Marie	1.01	1.01	1.01	0.97	0.91	0.95	1.02	0.98	1.05	1.
Sudbury	1.06	1.10	n/a	1.13	0.76	0.73	0.78	0.82	0.88	0.
Thunder Bay	0.87	0.85	0.91	0.94	0.90	0.87	0.96	0.98	0.97	0.
Toronto	1.12	1.08	1.11	1.11	1.03	1.03	1.01	n/a	1.09	1.
Windsor	0.97	1.04	1.02	1.00	0.99	0.74	0.91	0.97	0.99	0.
Woodstock	0.92	1.03	0.96	0.96	0.88	0.91	0.95	1.01	0.99	1.

1962	1963	1964	1965	1966	1967	1968	1969	1970	1971	1972	1973
1.01	0.95	0.93	0.94	0.92	0.96	0.97	1.06	1.04	1.05	0.98	1.04
n/a	1.00	0.97	0.93	0.97	1.01	1.04	1.09	1.07	1.07	0.98	0.96
1.08	1.03	1.07	1.10	1.10	1.11	1.07	1.05	1.03	0.99	0.96	0.99
0.91	1.02	0.95	1.01	1.06	1.09	1.06	1.10	1.00	1.06	1.09	1.20
0.86	0.90	0.95	0.89	0.96	0.88	0.93	0.90	0.93	0.93	1.05	1.06
1.09	1.09	1.14	1.14	1.09	1.27	1.22	1.19	1.18	1.18	1.18	1.12
0.99	0.98	1.06	1.21	1.11	1.07	1.03	1.06	1.07	1.11	1.12	1.07
1.15	1.15	1.13	1.22	1.30	1.18	1.22	1.14	1.07	1.13	1.17	1.09
1.20	1.19	1.25	1.31	1.42	1.20	1.14	1.21	1.19	1.18	1.31	1.19
1.09	1.09	1.23	1.18	1.25	1.25	1.24	1.19	1.10	1.12	1.13	1.24
1.05	1.05	1.06	1.04	1.10	1.04	1.14	1.15	1.13	1.08	1.08	1.05
1.15	1.15	1.08	1.08	1.08	1.13	1.15	1.17	1.26	1.26	1.21	1.22
1.14	1.08	0.96	1.09	1.02	1.11	1.07	1.03	1.02	0.98	0.89	1.08
0.96	0.95	0.99	0.96	0.96	0.97	1.02	0.95	0.96	0.98	1.14	1.12
1.05	1.07	1.10	1.09	1.03	1.06	1.11	1.09	1.10	1.04	1.14	1.18
0.91	0.94	0.95	0.90	0.96	1.10	1.07	1.07	1.03	1.03	1.05	1.12
1.04	1.01	1.01	1.00	1.05	1.03	1.12	1.14	1.13	1.05	1.08	1.16
1.05	1.05	1.06	1.08	1.06	1.12	1.12	1.15	1.12	1.11	1.03	1.14
0.99	1.01	1.00	1.00	1.00	1.05	1.09	1.13	1.02	1.10	1.16	1.05
0.96	0.96	0.97	0.92	0.92	1.07	1.14	1.16	1.21	1.31	1.38	1.25
1.12	1.11	1.04	1.01	1.01	1.04	1.14	1.18	1.21	1.14	1.22	1.21
1.11	1.03	1.08	1.11	1.07	1.07	1.11	1.15	1.14	1.15	1.16	1.07
0.99	0.96	0.95	0.94	0.99	0.99	1.00	1.01	1.06	1.04	1.01	0.99
0.97	0.97	0.97	0.98	0.94	0.96	0.93	1.00	0.92	0.91	0.92	0.93
1.02	1.03	1.08	1.05	1.03	1.01	1.00	1.03	1.02	1.01	0.98	1.03
0.91	0.90	0.90	0.90	0.88	0.90	0.97	1.03	1.00	1.01	0.93	1.00
0.94	0.95	1.01	0.99	0.98	1.04	1.04	1.03	0.98	1.10	1.12	1.07
1.16	1.16	1.14	1.16	1.11	1.19	1.21	1.19	1.24	1.22	1.22	1.13
0.98	0.99	0.96	0.96	0.94	1.07	1.09	1.08	1.06	1.09	1.08	1.12
0.99	0.99	1.01	1.00	1.05	1.10	1.22	1.06	1.06	1.06	1.12	1.05

Table 7 continued over

77

Table 7 (Ratio of Municipal/Private Average Wages of Labourers)
continued

Municipality	1952	1953	1954	1955	1956	1957	1958	1959	1960	196
Winnipeg	0.93	1.00	0.99	0.96	0.98	1.05	0.99	n/a	1.07	1.0
Regina	0.96	1.05	1.02	0.98	1.04	1.06	0.91	0.94	0.96	0.9
Saskatoon	0.81	0.95	0.92	0.92	0.96	0.95	0.93	0.94	1.00	0.9
Calgary	0.99	0.95	n/a	0.97	0.97	0.94	1.00	1.04	1.05	1.0
Edmonton	0.96	1.04	1.06	1.02	1.01	1.01	1.05	0.99	1.14	1.1
Vancouver	1.00	1.03	1.05	1.02	1.01	1.04	1.06	n/a	1.06	1.0
Victoria	0.91	0.89	0.91	0.89	0.91	0.87	0.85	0.87	1.02	1.0
Average	0.93	0.96	0.95	0.96	0.92	0.93	0.95	0.97	1.01	1.0

1962	1963	1964	1965	1966	1967	1968	1969	1970	1971	1972	1973
1.04	1.05	1.08	1.06	1.14	1.08	1.06	1.10	1.08	1.05	1.08	1.10
0.98	0.96	1.00	0.95	1.03	1.06	0.74	1.07	1.13	1.07	1.05	1.04
1.00	1.01	1.03	0.99	0.99	0.97	1.00	1.07	1.06	1.02	1.06	1.08
1.02	1.02	1.06	1.07	1.05	1.10	1.08	1.06	1.13	1.08	1.11	1.10
1.13	1.12	1.07	1.11	1.08	1.09	1.11	1.11	1.13	1.11	1.07	1.04
1.04	1.03	1.03	1.02	1.04	1.04	1.02	1.01	1.03	1.03	1.02	1.00
0.96	0.97	0.93	0.96	1.00	0.96	1.00	0.99	0.99	0.99	0.97	1.04
1.03	1.02	1.03	1.04	1.05	1.06	1.07	1.09	1.08	1.08	1.09	1.09

Source: Computed from data in *Wage Rates, Salaries and Hours of Labour,* Labour Canada, Economics and Research Branch, Surveys Division, Annual. The municipal data is from the industry wage section for municipal labourers (Table 90 or 91 for 1966-73, Table 82 for 1957-65, Table 83 for 1956, Table 82 for 1955, Table 12 for 1953-54, and Table 11 for 1952). The private sector data is from the community wage rate section (nonproduction labour, all industries for 1973, general labour all industries for 1960-72, and general labourer manufacturing for 1952-59). If only a range of wages was given then the midpoint was used as the average rate.

Reproduced here from Morley Gunderson, "Public-Private Wage and Non-Wage Differentials: Calculations from Published Tabulations," Institute for Research on Public Policy, 1977, pp. 14-15.

TABLE 8
Public/Private Pay Comparisons
October 1974

Occupation	Ottawa-Hull AllInd	Ottawa-Hull PubAd	Halifax-Dartmouth AllInd	Halifax-Dartmouth PubAd	Montreal AllInd	Montreal PubAd	Regina AllInd	Regina PubAd	Toronto AllInd	Toronto PubAd
Male Labourer										
Avg Hourly Wage ($)	3.78	3.93	3.55	3.66	3.73	4.09	3.65	3.25	3.94	4.51
Union rate ($)	(4.10)		(3.61)		(3.84)		(3.66)		(4.13)	
500+ employ ($)	(4.42)		(3.49)		(4.03)		(3.62)		(4.14)	
Avg Wkly Hrs	40.5	40.0	40.2	40.0	40.2	40.0	39.4	38.9	40.1	40.0
Female File Clerk										
Avg Wkly Salary ($)	114	145	98	109	97	135	99	117	111	120
Union rate ($)	(126)		(105)		(110)		(100)		(125)	
500+ employ ($)	(118)		(108)		(109)		(100)		(121)	
Avg Weekly Hrs	37.3	37.5	36.8	36.3	36.4	34.5	36.8	36.6	36.8	36.6
Female Manager										
Avg Weekly Salary ($)	249	283	279	—	214	296	—	—	222	287
Male Manager										
Avg Weekly Salary ($)	292	289		332	303	338	—	—	302	295

Source: *Wage Rates, Salaries, and Hours of Labour, 1974*, Labour Canada, Economics and Research Branch, Surveys Division.

TABLE 9
Public Sector Earnings Advantage and its Decomposition

	Overall Differential	Amount Attributed To	
		Endowments	Surplus
Males			
Dollar Advantage	737	245	492
As per cent of private earnings	9.3	3.1	6.2
As per cent of overall differential	100.0	33.4	66.6
Females			
Dollar Advantage	989	606	383
As per cent of private earnings	22.3	13.7	8.6
As per cent of overall differential	100.0	61.3	38.7

Source: Morley Gunderson, "Earnings Differentials Between the Public and Private Sectors," Institute for Policy Analysis, University of Toronto, p. 11.

TABLE 10

Value of Fringe Benefits,
Private, Provincial, and Municipal, 1976

Benefits	% of Payroll			$ per Employee/Yr.		
	Private	Prov.	Munic.	Private	Prov.	Munic.
All Employees						
Life insurance	.68	.37	.48	86	43	60
Health plans	1.23	1.29	1.06	146	146	128
Salary continuation	2.29	3.80	3.88	267	406	457
Legislated benefits	3.33	2.67	3.68	390	298	420
Vacations, holidays	10.33	10.54	10.33	1278	1164	1211
Pension plans	7.43	8.42	6.01	917	880	715
Total	25.29	27.09	25.44	3084	2937	2991
Office Employees						
Life insurance	.76	.36	.56	104	43	80
Health plans	1.18	1.23	1.04	153	140	140
Salary continuation	2.32	3.78	4.07	283	413	535
Legislated benefits	2.72	2.52	3.27	342	288	421
Vacations, holidays	10.12	10.48	10.81	1278	1181	1418
Pension plans	7.71	8.44	6.80	1011	901	898
Total	24.81	26.81	26.55	3171	2966	3492

Table 10 continued next page

Table 10 (Value of Fringe Benefits, Private, Provincial, and Municipal, 1976) *continued*

Benefits	% of Payroll			$ per Employee/Yr.		
	Private	**Prov.**	**Munic.**	**Private**	**Prov.**	**Munic.**
Non-Office Employees						
Life insurance	.58	.40	.42	64	45	44
Health plans	1.29	1.45	1.08	137	160	117
Salary continuation	2.26	3.83	3.72	245	389	393
Legislated benefits	3.99	3.07	4.00	441	322	419
Vacations, holidays	10.55	10.70	9.96	1175	1119	1052
Pension plans	7.12	8.37	5.34	809	827	560
Total	25.79	27.82	24.52	2871	2862	2564

Note: These figures are simply arithmetic totals of the expenditure on the packages and should *not* be taken to represent expenditure on a "total benefit package."

Source: Private sector figures are from *Employee Benefits and Conditions of Employment in Canada,* Ottawa: Pay Research Bureau, 1977, p. 104; Provincial and Municipal figures are from *Benefits and Working Conditions 1976,* Vol. 4, Ottawa: Pay Research Bureau, 1976, p. 14, 16, 42, and 44. Reproduced from Morley Gunderson, "Public-Private Wage and Non-Wage Differentials: Calculations from Published Tabulations," Institute for Research on Public Policy, p. 31.

TABLE 11

Collective Bargaining Legislation for Public Employees
as of January 1, 1978

Jurisdiction	Civil Servants	Teachers	Police	Firefighters	Hospital Workers
Federal:	strike	strike	no collec. bargaining	strike	strike
Provincial:					
Alta.	arbitration	strike	arbitration	arbitration	strike
B.C.	strike	arbitration	strike	strike	strike
Man.	arbitration	arbitration	arbitration	arbitration	strike
N.B.	strike	strike	arbitration	arbitration	strike
Nfld.	strike	strike	arbitration	arbitration	arbitration
N.S.	arbitration	strike	strike	strike	strike
Ont.	arbitration	strike	arbitration	arbitration	arbitration
P.E.I.	arbitration	arbitration	arbitration	arbitration	arbitration
Que.	strike	strike	arbitration	arbitration	strike
Sask.	strike	arbitration	strike	strike	strike

Sources: Collective Bargaining Legislation for Special Groups, Labour Canada, Legislative Research Branch, 1975; "Labour Legislation in Canada, 1975;" *Labour Gazette,* March 1976, February 1977, and May 1977; Goldenberg (1979), pp. 254-255.

NOTES

1   See Beaucage, p. 14, and various annual editions of *Labour Organization in Canada.*

2   In Canada, once a union is certified as the collective bargaining agent for a designated group of employees, the agent has exclusive jurisdiction over all employees in that bargaining unit, whether or not they are union members. Hence, unless the union negotiates a union or closed shop, thereby compelling all employees in the bargaining unit to join the union, there may be some non-union employees who will be covered by the collective agreement.

3   *Labour Gazette,* December, 1977, p. 563.

4   Beaucage, p. 21.

5   The figures presented in Tables 4.a and 4.b do not include the communication sector in the public sector counts. However, when this is done, there is no reason for a difference in conclusions drawn, as can be seen by comparing Table 4.b to the one below:

Work Stoppages Per Unionized Employee

Public Sector (Including Communication)
as a Percentage of the Whole Economy

Period	Number of stoppages	Number of workers involved	Man-days lost
1960-64	21.2	15.4	7.1
1965-69	28.6	89.7	43.2
1970-74	34.4	94.3	38.0

Source: Table 3.b; *Union Growth in Canada in the Sixties,* Table 1, pp. 16-17, Labour Canada, Economics and Research Branch; and *Labour Gazette,* December 1977, p. 563.

6   Fogel and Lewin (1974), p. 413.

7   Doherty (1975), p. 711.

8   Fogel and Lewin (1974), p. 413.

9   Reisman (1977), p. 16; Goldenberg (1979), p. 265.

10   Cousineau and Lacroix (1977) present the following figures showing the relative dearth of COLA clauses in the public sector on p. 15 of their study entitled *Wage Determination in Major Collective Agreements in the Private and Public Sectors.*

Proportion of Major Collective Agreements With COLA Clauses,
Private and Public Sectors,

1971-75

Year	Total	Private	Public
1971	4.4	6.0	n/a
1972	11.8	13.6	7.4
1973	19.4	23.6	9.5
1974	33.7	40.5	17.7
1975	41.0	50.4	20.3

Source: Unpublished Labour Canada statistics estimates by the authors.

11   Gunderson (1977 c), p. 1.
12   Gunderson (1977 b), p. 9.
13   Gunderson (1978), p. 15.
14   Ibid., p. 12.
15   Morley (1977), pp. 7-8.
16   See MacIntosh (1976).
17   Gunderson (1977 c), p. 29.
18   Ibid.
19   See Morley (1977) and Wilkins (1974).
20   See Goldenberg (1979), p. 275.
21   During the 1977-78 session of Parliament, the government introduced Bill C-28, an act to amend the *Public Service Staff Relations Act.* The bill died at the close of that session, but was reintroduced during the 1978-79 session as Bill C-22. This too died at the dissolution of Parliament. The principle amendments proposed were the following:
   a) The category of employees to be excluded from bargaining under the act would be redefined to include not only employees working in a managerial or confidential capacity, but also those employees earning $33,500 or more per year. This income criterion would be subject to review by the Cabinet in conjunction with changes in salary levels in the Public Service.
   b) It would be forbidden for any collective agreement to provide for a maximum salary that would be equal to or higher than the dollar figure specified in (a).
   c) An Advisory Committee for the Pay Research Bureau would be established, to be composed of both employer and employee representatives.
   d) It would be required that arbitral awards be accompanied by an explanation of the factors considered in reaching a decision.
   e) Arbitration tribunals would be explicitly instructed that one of the factors they must consider in making an award is the attainment or maintenance of parity with the aggregate of compensation received for comparable work in the profit-making sector of the economy.
   f) The public employer would, under specified circumstances, be permitted to lockout his employees in the process of collective bargaining.

Further, he would be permitted to layoff, for up to 60 days, any employee idled by the strike action of others.

g) If Parliament were not in session, the Cabinet would have the authority to order a cooling-off period of up to 21 days if a threatened strike or lockout would adversely affect the national interest.

22   Arthurs (1971), Chapter III.

23   Woods (1973), Chapter 8.

24   Barnes and Kelly (1975), p. 11, and *Labour Gazette,* August 1978, pp. 339-340.

25   Anderson and Kochan (1977), p. 292.

26   Barnes and Kelly (1975), p. 11.

27   Finkelman, Part I, p. 158.

28   Ibid., p. 160.

29   Ibid., p. 162.

30   Barnes and Kelly (1975), p. 3. See also Armstrong (1968).

31   Wellington and Winter (1972), p. 191.

32   Ibid., Chapter 1.

33   Cousineau and Lacroix (1977), p. 62. It should be noted that the results obtained by Cousineau and Lacroix are contradicted by the results of a later study on the same data base authored by Auld, Christofides, Swidinsky and Wilton (ACSW). In the results ACSW presented in their work for the Anti-Inflation Board, they found no significant difference between public and private sectors in the determinants of wage settlements (ACSW, 1979a, p. 194). When ACSW eliminated those public sector settlements reached via arbitration, they found a significant difference between public and private sectors, with the surprising result that the public sector was *more* responsive to market conditions than the private sector (ACSW, 1979b, p. 200). Neither of these findings are given much credence here because of what appears to be a misuse of data in the ACSW studies. ACSW used the regionalized help-wanted index, published by the Department of Finance, as their labour market demand variable. However, because the index is normalized at 100 for 1969 for each region, comparison of these index values *across* regions is meaningless. Hence, the ACSW estimates for both public and private sector wage equations are suspect.

There may also be a problem with the estimates by Cousineau and Lacroix, due to their inclusion of contracts with COLA clauses in their data sample. This means that some of the dependent variable values are measured inaccurately and since this measurement error will be correlated with the rate of inflation (one of the explanatory variables), the resultant estimates will be biased. The dummy variable used by Cousineau and Lacroix to control for the existence of a COLA clause in the contract mitigates but probably does not eliminate the problem entirely.

34   Ibid., p. 65.

35   Ibid., p. 66.

36   See Hodgetts *et al.* (1972), ch. 13-14, for a full discussion of the factors leading to the introduction of collective bargaining in the federal public service.

37 See Gunderson (1977 a).

38 See Goldenberg (1979), p. 285, for evidence of the chilling effect in the federal public service.

39 Burton and Krider (1975), p. 171.

40 Wellington and Winter (1972), p. 195.

41 See Courchene (1977).

42 Wellington and Winter (1972), p. 198.

43 Ibid.

44 Ibid.

45 Ibid., p. 200.

46 The proposed wage boards would perform the same type of research as is currently done in the federal sector by the Pay Research Bureau. However, unlike the Pay Research Bureau, they would have the authority to set compensation levels.

47 See Finn (1971).

48 In their study on the determinants of wage settlements, Auld *et al.* (1979 a) claim that they find no evidence of spillovers from public sector wage settlements to those in the private sector. If there were no spillover effects at all, then the arguments made in this paragraph would be unfounded. However, there are two things to note about the Auld *et al.* findings: 1) They test only for spillovers that take the form of comparable *realized* wage increases. Even if the private sector fails to achieve comparable wage increases, the labour unrest and unemployment that result from private sector attempts to achieve comparable increases are still a threat, and there is ample news media evidence to indicate that such attempts are made. 2) The method Auld *et al.* used to determine whether there were realized wage spillover effects is weak, since they looked only for spillovers from public to private sectors within regions, without disaggregating by occupation. A realistic test would have to look for spillovers from wage settlements for clerical workers in the public sector to clerical workers in the private sector, etc.

49 See Gunderson (1977 a) for a discussion of this issue.

50 See Auld *et al.* (1979 b); Cousineau and Lacroix (1978).

51 See Reisman (1977), p. 16.

BIBLIOGRAPHY

Anderson, J. and T. Kochan (1977). "Impasse Procedures in the Canadian Federal Service: Effects of the Bargaining Process," *Industrial and Labor Relations Review,* 30:3, pp. 283-301.

Armstrong, Robert (1968). "Some Aspects of Policy Determination in the Development of the Collective Bargaining Legislation in the Public Service of Canada," *Canadian Public Administration,* 11:4, pp. 485-493.

Arthurs, Harry (1971). *Collective Bargaining by Public Employees in Canada: Five Models,* Ann Arbor, Michigan, Institute of Labor & Industrial Relations, University of Michigan.

Ashenfelter, O. and G.E. Johnson (1969). "Bargaining Theory, Trade Unions, and Industrial Strike Activity," *American Economic Review,* 59, pp. 35-49.

Ashenfelter, O. and G.E. Johnson (1972). "Unionism, Relative Wages and Labor Quality in U.S. Manufacturing Industries," *International Economic Review,* 13:3, pp. 488-508.

Auld, D., L. Christofides, R. Swidinsky, and D. Wilton (1979 a). *The Determinants of Negotiated Wage Settlements in Canada (1966-1975),* Anti-Inflation Board.

Auld, D., L. Christofides, R. Swidinsky, and D. Wilton (1979 b). "The Impact of the Anti-Inflation Board on Negotiated Wage Settlements," *Canadian Journal of Economics,* 12:2, pp. 195-213.

Barnes, L.W.C.S. and L.A. Kelly (1975). "Interest Arbitration in the Federal Public Service of Canada," Research and Current Issues Series No. 31, Industrial Relations Centre, Queens University.

Beaucage, Andre (1976). *An Outline of the Canadian Labour Relations System,* Labour Canada, Employment Relations Branch.

Becker, G. (1971). *The Economics of Discrimination,* University of Chicago Press, 2nd edition.

Brittan, S. (1976). "The Political Economy of British Union Monopoly," *Three Banks Review,* 111, pp. 3-32.

Bromstein, Reuben M. (1970). "Must an Individual Union Member's Rights Be Sacrificed to Protect the Group Interest?" *Relations Industrielles,* 25:2, pp. 325-344.

Bronfenbrenner, M. (1958). "The Incidence of Collective Bargaining Once More," *Southern Economic Journal,* 24, pp. 398-406.

Buchanan, J. and G. Tullock (1962). *The Calculus of Consent,* Ann Arbor, University of Michigan Press.

Burstein, M. *et al.* (1975?. *Canadian Work Values: Findings of a Work Ethic Survey and a Job Satisfaction Survey.* Ottawa, Department of Manpower and Immigration.

Burton and Krider (1970). "The Role and Consequences of Strikes by Public Employees," *Yale Law Journal,* 79:3, pp. 418-440.

Burton and Krider (1975). "The Incidence of Strikes in Public Employment," pp. 135-177, in *Labour in the Public and Non-Profit Sectors,* edited by Daniel Hamermesh.

Carr, J. *et al.* (1976). *The Illusion of Wage and Price Control,* Vancouver, The Fraser Institute.

Christie, Innis and Morley Gorsky (1968). *Unfair Labour Practices,* Task Force on Labour Relations, Study No. 10.

Courchene, Thomas J. (1977). "Post Controls and the Public Sector," pp. 143-181, in Douglas Auld *et al., Which Way Ahead?,* Vancouver, The Fraser Institute.

Cousineau, Jean-Michel and Robert Lacroix (1977). *Wage Determination in Major Collective Agreements in the Private and Public Sectors,* Economic Council of Canada.

Cousineau, Jean-Michel and Robert Lacroix (1978). "L'Impact de la Politique canadienne de controle des prix et des revenue sur les ententes salariales," *Canadian Public Policy,* 4:1, pp. 88-100.

Crispo, John (1971). "Industrial Relations in Western Europe and Canada," in Industrial Relations Research Association, *A Review of Industrial Relations Research, Volume II,* pp. 210-216.

Crispo, John (1978). *The Canadian Industrial Relations System,* Toronto, McGraw-Hill Ryerson.

Davidson, P. and S. Weintraub (1973). "Money as Cause and Effect," *Economic Journal,* pp. 1117-1132.

Diewert, Erwin (1974). "The Effects of Unionization on Wages and Employment: A General Equilibrium Analysis," *Economic Inquiry,* 12:3, pp. 319-339.

Doherty, William (1975). "The Government as Employer," *Labour Gazette,* October, pp. 711-715.

Eaton, B.C. (1972). "The Worker and the Profitability of the Strike," *Industrial and Labor Relations Review,* 26:1, pp. 670-679.

Economic Council of Canada (1973). *Shaping the Expansion,* Tenth Annual Review, Ottawa, Information Canada.

Economic Council of Canada (1974). *Economic Targets and Social Indicators,* Eleventh Annual Review, Ottawa, Information Canada.

Economic Council of Canada (1976). *People and Jobs: A Study of the Canadian Labour Market,* Ottawa, Information Canada.

Evans, J. and G. MacDonald (1976). "On Estimating the Union-Nonunion Wage Differential in Canada," mimeo.

Finkelman, J. (1974). *Employer-Employee Relations in the Public Service of Canada, Parts I and II,* Ottawa, Information Canada.

Finn, E. (1971). "Resolving Industrial Strife: Is There a 'Better Way'?," *Labour Gazette,* December, pp. 774-783.

Fleisher, B. (1970). *Labour Economics: Theory and Evidence,* Prentice-Hall, Englewood Cliffs, New Jersey.

Fogel and Lewin (1974). "Wage Determination in the Public Sector," *Industrial and Labor Relations Review,* 27:3, pp. 410-431.

Galbraith, J. (1967). *The New Industrial State,* New York, Signet Books.

Goldenberg, S. (1979). "Public-Sector Labor Relations in Canada," in B. Aaron, J.R. Grodin , and J.L. Stern (editors), *Public-Sector Bargaining,* Industrial Relations Research Association Series, pp. 254-291.

Gordon, R.J. (1976). "Recent Developments in the Theory of Inflation and Unemployment," *Journal of Monetary Economics,* 2, pp. 185-219.

Green, C. and J.M. Cousineau (1976). *Unemployment in Canada: The Impact of Unemployment Insurance,* Ottawa, Economic Council of Canada.

Gunderson, Morley, ed. (1975). *Collective Bargaining in the Essential and Public Service Sectors,* Toronto, University of Toronto Press.

Gunderson, Morley (1977a). "Criteria for Public Sector Wage Determination," Anti-Inflation Board Discussion Paper.

Gunderson, Morley (1977b). "Public-Private Sector Differences and Implications for Wage Determination," Anti-Inflation Board, Research Branch.

Gunderson, Morley (1977c). "Public-Private Wage and Non-wage Differentials: Calculations from Published Tabulations," Institute for Research on Public Policy. A revised version of this has been published in D.K. Foot, ed., *Public Employment and Compensation in Canada,* Toronto, Butterworths, 1978, pp. 127-166.

Gunderson, Morley (1978). "Earnings Differentials Between the Public and Private Sectors," Institute for Policy Analysis, University of Toronto. A shorter version of this is published in *Canadian Journal of Economics,* 12:2 (May 1979), pp. 228-242.

Hall, Robert (1975). "The Rigidity of Wages and the Persistence of Unemployment," *Brookings Papers on Economic Activity,* 2:1975.

Hanslowe, Kent L. (1963). "The Collective Agreement and the Duty of Fair Representation," *Labor Law Journal,* pp. 1052-1072.

Herberg, Will (1972). "Bureaucracy and Democracy in Labour Unions," in Richard L. Rowan, ed., *Readings in Labor Economics and Labor Relations,* pp. 232-239.

Hicks, J. (1932). *The Theory of Wages,* New York, Macmillan.

Hodgetts, J.E. *et al.* (1972). *The Biography of an Institution: The Civil Service Commission of Canada, 1908-1967,* Montreal, McGill-Queen's University Press.

Horsfall, R. *et al.* (1974). "Parameters of Healthful Community and Individual Functioning in Resource Frontier Towns," Department of Economics and Commerce, Simon Fraser University, mimeo.

Hotson, J. (1971). "Adverse Effect of Tax and Interest Hikes as Strengthening the Case for Incomes Policies—Or a Part of the Elephant," *Canadian Journal of Economics,* 4:2, pp. 164-181.

Jamieson, S. (1973). *Industrial Relations in Canada,* 2nd edition, Toronto, Macmillan.

Johnson, G. (1975). "Economic Analysis of Trade Unionism," *American Economic Review,* 65:2, pp. 23-28.

Johnson, H. and P. Mieszkowski (1970). "The Effects of Unionization on the Distribution of Income: A General Equilibrium Approach," *Quarterly Journal of Economics,* pp. 539-561.

Jones, J. and L. Laudadio (1975). "Wage Differentials and Market Imperfections: Some Cross Section Results in Canadian Manufacturing Industries," *Relations Industrielles,* 30:3, pp. 408-421.

Katzner, Donald W. and Sidney Weintraub (1974), "An Approach to a Unified Micro-Macro Economic Model," *Kyklos,* 27:3, pp. 482-510.

Labour Canada (1967a). *The Behaviour of Canadian Wages and Salaries in the Post-War Period,* Ottawa.

Labour Canada (1967b). *Forty-Two Provisions in Major Collective Agreements Covering Employees in Canadian Manufacturing Industries,* Ottawa.

Labour Canada (1968). *Provisions in Collective Agreements Covering Employees in Canadian Mining Industries,* Ottawa.

Labour Canada (1969). *Provisions in Major Collective Agreements in Canadian Manufacturing Industries,* Ottawa.

Labour Canada (1974). *Provisions in Major Collective Agreements Covering Employees in Canadian Manufacturing Industries,* Ottawa.

Labour Canada (1975). *Collective Bargaining Legislation for Special Groups in Canada,* Legislative Research Branch, Analysis and Evaluation Division.

Labour Canada (1975). *Provisions in Major Collective Agreements Covering Employees in Certain Transportation, Communications, Trade, Utilities, and Service Industries in Canada,* Ottawa.

Labour Canada. *Labour Gazette,* various monthly issues.

Labour Canada. *Labour Organizations in Canada, 1974-75.*

Labour Canada. *Strikes and Lockouts in Canada,* Economics and Research Branch, various annual issues.

Labour Canada. *Union Growth in Canada, 1921-1967,* Economics and Research Branch.

Labour Canada. *Union Growth in Canada in the Sixties,* Economics and Research Branch.

Labour Canada. *Wage Rates, Salaries, and Hours of Labour,* Economics and Research Branch, Surveys Division, various annual issues.

Labour Canada. *Working Conditions in Canadian Industry.* Economic and Research Branch, Surveys Division, various annual issues.

Laidler, D. (1976). "An Alternative to Wage and Price Controls," in J. Carr et al., *The Illusion of Wage and Price Control,* Vancouver, The Fraser Institute, pp. 179-210.

Leiserson, W. (1931). "The Economics of the Restriction of Output," in S. Mathewson, ed., *Restrictions of Output Among Unorganized Workers,* Antioch College.

Lewis, H.G. (1963). *Unionism and Relative Wages in the United States,* University of Chicago Press.

Lewis, H.G. (1964). "Relative Employment Effects of Unionism," Proceedings, 16th Annual Winter Meeting, Industrial Relations Research Association, Boston, December 27-28, 1963, pp. 104-115.

MacIntosh, R.M. (1976). "The Great Pension Fund Robbery," *Canadian Public Policy,* Spring, pp. 256-262.

MacMillan, J. et al. (1974). *Determinants of Labour Turnover in Canadian Mining Communities,* Centre for Settlement Studies, University of Manitoba, Series 2, Research Report No. 19.

Malles, P. (1975). *Employment Insecurity and Industrial Relations in the Canadian Construction Industry,* Ottawa, Economic Council of Canada.

Malles, P. (1976). *Canadian Labour Standards in Law, Agreements, and Practice,* Ottawa, Economic Council of Canada.

Maxwell, Judith (1976). *Policy Review and Outlook: Challenges to Complacency,* C.D. Howe Research Institute.

Miernyk, W. (1965). *The Economics of Labor and Collective Bargaining,* Boston, D.C. Heath.

Miller, R. (1976). "Right-to-Work Laws and Compulsory Union Membership in the United States," *British Journal of Industrial Relations,* 14:2.

Morgenstern, P. (1963). *On the Accuracy of Economic Observations,* Princeton University Press.

Morley, D. (1977). "Managerial Compensation in the Federal Public Service," paper presented at the Third Canadian Compensation Conference, Toronto.

Nightingale, D. (1975). "Work Ethic is Alive and Well in Quebec," *Financial Post,* June 28.

Ostry, S. and M. Zaidi (1972). *Labour Economics in Canada,* 2nd edition, Toronto, Macmillan.

Palomba, N. and C. Palomba (1971). "Right-to-Work Laws: A Suggested Economic Rationale," *Journal of Law and Economics,* 14:2, pp. 475-483.

Peitchinis, S. (1972). "Evolution of the Canadian Wage and Salary Structure," Department of Economics, University of Guelph, mimeo.

Peitchinis, S. (1975). *The Canadian Labour Market,* Toronto, Oxford University Press.

Pratten, C.F. (1976). *Labour Productivity Differentials within International Companies,* Cambridge University Press.

Rees, A. (1948). *Trade Unions Wage Policy,* University of California Press.

Rees, A. (1962). *The Economics of Trade Unions,* University of Chicago Press.

Rees, A. (1963). "The Effects of Unions on Resource Allocation," *Journal of Law and Economics,* 6, pp. 69-78.

Reisman, Simon S. (1977). "Controls: The Great Fallacy," in *Which Way Ahead?,* Vancouver, The Fraser Institute, pp. 5-19.

Schmidt, P. and R.P. Strauss (1976). "The Effect of Unions on Earnings and Earnings on Unions: A Mixed Logit Approach," *International Economic Review,* 17:1, pp. 204-212.

Sharir, S. (1978). "On Union Security and 'Right-to-Work' Legislation with Special Reference to Canada: An Economist's View," Department of Economics, University of Alberta, Discussion Paper 78-12.

Soutar, D. (1974). "Co-Determination, Industrial Democracy, and the Role of Management," Proceedings, Twenty-sixth Annual Winter Meeting, Industrial Relations Research Association, New York, December 28-29, 1973, pp. 1-7.

Starr, G. (1973). *Union-Nonunion Wage Differentials: A Cross-sectional Analysis, Research Branch,* Ontario Ministry of Labour.

Statistics Canada. *Aggregate Productivity Measures* (14-201), Ottawa, various issues.

94

Statistics Canada. *Canadian Statistical Review* (11-;;3), various monthly issues, Ottawa.

Statistics Canada. *Canadian Statistical Review, Historical Summary 1970* (11-505), Ottawa.

Statistics Canada. *Corporations and Labour Unions Returns Act, Part II, Labour Unions* (71-202), Ottawa, various issues.

Statistics Canada. *Historical Labour Force Statistics, 1974* (71-201), Ottawa.

Statistics Canada. *System of National Accounts, National Income and Expenditure Accounts, Volume I, The Annual Estimates, 1926-1974* (13-531), Ottawa.

Swidinsky, R. (1972). "Trade Unions and the Rate of Change of Money Wages in Canada, 1953-1970," *Industrial and Labor Relations Review,* 25:3, pp. 207-221.

Swidinsky, R. (1976). "Strike Settlement and Economic Activity: An Empirical Analysis," *Relations Industrielles,* 31:2, pp. 207-221.

Turner, H.A. (1952). "Trade Unions, Differentials, and the Leveling of Wages," *The Manchester School of Economics and Social Studies,* 20:1, pp. 227-282.

Walker, M. (1976). "Some Questions and Answers about Inflation," in J. Carr *et al., The Illusion of Wage and Price Control,* Vancouver, The Fraser Institute, pp. 215-236.

Walsh, William D. (1975). "Economic Conditions and Strike Activity in Canada," *Industrial Relations,* 14, pp. 45-54.

Weintraub, S. (1971). "An Incomes Policy to Stop Inflation," *Lloyds Bank Review,* January, pp. 1-12.

Weintraub, S. (1974). "A Theory of Monetary Policy under Wage Inflation," Australia and New Zealand Banking group Limited Research Lecture, University of Queensland Press.

Wellington, Harry and Ralph Winter (1972). *The Unions and the Cities,* Washington, D.C., The Brookings Institution.

Wilkins, J. (1974). "Senior Salary Levels in Government," *Canadian Business Review,* Spring, pp. 41-44.

Williamson, O.E., M.L. Wachter, and J.E. Harris (1975). "Understanding the Employment Relation: The Analysis of Idiosyncratic Exchange," *Bell Journal of Economics,* 6:1, pp. 250-280.

Woods, H.D. (1968). *Canadian Industrial Relations,* Report of the Task Force on Labour Relations, Ottawa, Privy Council Office.

Woods, H.D. (1973). *Labour Policy in Canada,* 2nd edition, Toronto, Macmillan.

THE FRASER INSTITUTE
Member of the Association of Canadian Publishers
and the Canadian Booksellers Association

Books on Current Economic Issues

PRIVATIZATION: THEORY AND PRACTICE
Distributing Shares in Private and Public Enterprises:
BCRIC, PETROCAN, ESOPs, GSOPs

In March 1979, the government of British Columbia launched a unique, new experiment in economic policy by divesting itself of the ownership of the British Columbia Resources Investment Corporation and giving the shares to the citizens of British Columbia.

T. M. Ohashi, Senior Vice President and Director of Research, Pemberton Securities Limited, Vancouver, provides for the first time the real story of how BCRIC was born as a private, widely-held corporation. He also provides an analysis of the largest common stock offering in Canadian history (which was made at the same time as the "giveaway"), who bought it, and what impact it has had on Canada's financial markets.

In the second part of the book, **T. P. Roth**, Chairman of the Department of Economics and Finance at the University of Texas at El Paso and a Senior Economist with the U.S. Congress Joint Economic Committee's Special Study on Economic Change in Washington, D.C., examines the effects of Generalized Stock Ownership Plans, particularly of the sort espoused by Louis O. Kelso. Given that some of the claims made by Kelso have been repeated by those who support BCRIC-type experiments, it is important at this time to re-examine his ideas. Also included is a theoretical overview of privatization and the public interest by **Zane Spindler**, an Associate Professor of Economics at Simon Fraser University in B.C., as well as an analysis of the prospects for privatizing the Alberta Heritage Savings Trust Fund by **Melville McMillan** and **Kenneth Norrie**, both Associate Professors of Economics at the University of Alberta in Edmonton.

256 pages extensive bibliographical notes $12.95 paperback ISBN 0-88975-036-X

TAX FACTS
The Canadian Consumer Tax Index and YOU

A major Fraser Institute book showing how the consumer tax burden in Canada has risen dramatically in recent years. Topics covered include *The Canadian Tax System; Personal Income Taxation in Canada; How Much Tax Do You Really Pay?; The Consumer Tax Index;* and *The Relative Burden of Taxation.*

By **Sally Pipes**, an Economist at the Fraser Institute, and **Michael Walker**, the Institute's Director, "Tax Facts" is a unique and highly readable analysis of the extent of direct and indirect taxation in Canada. In the case of some Canadians, hidden taxes make up more than 60 per cent of their tax bill. How much hidden tax do **you** pay? Do you want to know? Can you afford not to know!

The book contains a glossary of commonly-used terms, bibliographical notes and tables. It is an up-to-date sequel to the Institute's previous best-selling book "How Much Tax Do You Really Pay?"

140 pages   9 charts   29 tables $3.95 paperback   ISBN 0-88975-027-0

Fraser Institute Books in Print

THE HEALTH CARE BUSINESS
International Evidence on Private Versus Public Health Care Systems

Professor Åke Blomqvist, Associate Professor of Economics, University of Western Ontario, having studied the health care systems in Canada, the U.S., Britain and Sweden, recommends sweeping changes to Canada's system of medical insurance in *The Health Care Business*. In the process of ensuring equity in access to medical services, Blomqvist contends, the current Canadian system has become unacceptably inefficient and costly. The response of government to rising costs has been to increasingly intervene in the market for health services — gradually moving the Canadian system closer to the British system of "choice by bureaucrats". In the opinion of Professor Blomqvist, the result of this trend could well be a substantial reduction in the effectiveness of Canada's health service system — currently among the best in the world.

The Health Care Business sets out a series of changes to current medical and hospital insurance schemes in Canada which would have the effect, over time, of reducing the built-in cost escalation without materially affecting access to medical care. Blomqvist's recommendations are aimed at increasing competition amongst suppliers of medical services, breaking the conflict of interest that medical practitioners currently find themselves in and establishing an economically realistic basis for the delivery of hospital services.

208 pages   7 tables $5.95 paperback   ISBN 0-88975-026-2

THE SCIENCE COUNCIL'S WEAKEST LINK
A Critique of the Science Council's Technocratic Industrial Strategy for Canada

The Science Council of Canada recently published a study by two of its researchers — "The Weakest Link" — which purports to prove that the root of the country's economic malaise can be found in the "technological underdevelopment of Canadian industry." One solution, the Council's book proposes, is the adoption of an "Industrial Strategy" based on "technological sovereignty" involving wide-ranging and potentially massive intervention by government in the country's industrial structure.

Because the Science Council's views on Industrial Strategy are acquiring increasing attention in government policy circles and what many believe to be a credibility that is undeserved, this Fraser Institute book, by **Kristian Palda**, a Queen's University Professor of Business Economics, represents a searching critique of what is becoming the "Science Council view"; as such, it is a particularly useful contribution to the on-going debate about one of the most fundamental issues of our time.

73 pages   6 charts   7 tables $4.95 paperback   ISBN 0-88975-031-9

CANADIAN CONFEDERATION AT THE CROSSROADS
The Search for a Federal-Provincial Balance

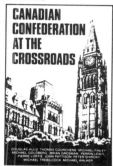

The eleven Fraser Institute authors examine carefully the extent to which the current allocation of powers and functions in the Canadian system of government serves the economic and cultural interests of all Canadians. Since the issues raised involve many aspects of our society, the book spans the broad mosaic of Canadian life from economic policy to legal uniformity; from broadcasting to urban development policy.

Canadian Confederation at the Crossroads: The Search for a Federal-Provincial Balance asks whether much of what is interpreted as **separatist** sentiment in Quebec in fact represents a deeply-rooted reaction to a rising feeling of alienation from government: a reaction as strongly rooted in the West and the Maritimes as in Quebec. As a solution, this book therefore looks at the ways personal and regional independence can be achieved within the framework of our existing constitutional structure. Can we produce a workable and acceptable federal-provincial balance that will reinvigorate our confederation?

Authors include: **Michael Walker**, Director, the Fraser Institute (Introduction); **Perrin Lewis**, Assistant Economic Adviser, Bank of Nova Scotia, Toronto (on the tangled tale of taxes and transfers); **John C. Pattison**, Assistant Professor, School of Business Administration, University of Western Ontario (on dividing the power to regulate); **Thomas J. Courchene**, Professor of Economics, University of Western Ontario (on the transfer system and regional disparities); **Peter Shiroky**, Fraser & Beatty, Toronto and **Michael Trebilcock**, Director, Law & Economics Programme, University of Toronto (on the uniformity of law); **Pierre Lortie**, Executive Vice-President, SECOR, Inc., Montreal (on education, broadcasting, and language policy); **Douglas A. Auld**, Professor of Economics, University of Guelph (on fiscal policy); **Brian A. Grosman**, Professor of Law, University of Saskatchewan and **Michael J. Finley**, Legal Research Officer, Law Reform Commission of Saskatchewan (on law enforcement); and **Michael A. Goldberg**, Professor & Chairman, Urban Land Economics Division, Faculty of Commerce & Business Administration, University of British Columbia (on housing and urban development policy).

381 pages	33 pages of extensive notes and bibliographical references	
10 tables	$9.95 paperback	ISBN 0-88975-025-4

FRIEDMAN ON GALBRAITH
...and on curing the British Disease

Why is it that **John Kenneth Galbraith's** theories have become widely accepted by the general public when there is almost a total lack of support for them in the economics profession? Is Galbraith a *scientist or a missionary*? **Milton Friedman**, Nobel Laureate in Economics 1976, addresses these and other questions about Galbraith as economist and prophet in this Fraser Institute book. Whatever the reader's view of Galbraith, this book by Friedman is must reading. It is said that Canada and other countries are on the same path as Britain — to some, the *British Disease* is the logical ending of Galbraith's story. In the second essay in this book, Professor Friedman outlines a cure for the British Disease: the principles that Friedman develops in this essay are of immediate Canadian interest as they point out the necessity to adopt gradualist corrective policies *now* before the more jarring policies currently required in the U.K. are necessary here.

66 pages	$3.95 paperback	ISBN 0-88975-015-7

OIL IN THE SEVENTIES
Essays on Energy Policy

Edited by **G. Campbell Watkins**, President, DataMetrics Limited, Calgary and Visiting Professor of Economics, University of Calgary and **Michael Walker**, Director of the Fraser Institute.

In Part One, *Energy in the Marketplace*, contributors include **Russell S. Uhler** of the University of British Columbia (on economic concepts of petroleum energy supply); **Ernst R. Berndt** of the University of British Columbia (on Canadian energy demand and economic growth); and **G. Campbell Watkins** (on Canadian oil and gas pricing).

In Part Two, *Government in the Marketplace*, contributors include **Walter J. Mead** of the University of California, Santa Barbara (on private enterprise, regulation and government enterprise in the energy sector); and **Edward W Erickson** of North Carolina State University and **Herbert S. Winokur, Jr.**, of Harvard University (on international oil and multi-national corporations).

In Part Three, *Oil in the Seventies: Policies and Prospects,* contributors include **G. David Quirin** and **Basil A. Kalymon**, both of the University of Toronto (on the financial position of the petroleum industry) and **James W. McKie** of the University of Texas at Austin (on United States and Canadian energy policy).

320 pages	17 charts	25 tables	index
$9.95 hardcover			ISBN 0-88975-018-1

THE ILLUSION OF WAGE AND PRICE CONTROL
Essays on Inflation, its Causes and its Cures

A look at the causes of inflation and an examination of responses to it in Canada, the United States, and the United Kingdom. Contributors include **Jack Carr, Michael Darby, Jackson Grayson, David Laidler, Michael Parkin, Robert Schuettinger** and **Michael Walker**.

258 pages	16 charts	7 tables	$2.95 pocketbook	ISBN 0-88975-005-X

WHICH WAY AHEAD?
Canada after Wage and Price Control

This book draws together the research and ideas of fifteen well-informed Canadian economists. It presents a remarkable concurrence of views on the controls programme, its effectiveness and on the causes of inflation. The book suggests policies best suited to give Canada a healthy and internationally-competitive economy. It discusses the need for restraint in the public sector; it proposes policies to meet the critical double-headed challenge of low inflation and full employment. Contributors are: **Douglas Auld, Jack Carr, Louis Christofides, Thomas Courchene, James W. Dean, John Floyd, Herbert Grubel, John Helliwell, Stephan Kaliski, David Laidler, Richard Lipsey, Michael Parkin, Simon Reisman, Grant Reuber** and **Michael Walker**.

376 pages	5 charts	9 tables	$4.95 paperback	ISBN 0-88975-010-6

Books on Labour Market Issues

UNEMPLOYMENT INSURANCE
Global Evidence of its Effects on Unemployment

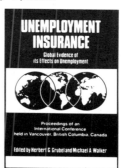

This book contains thirteen papers originally presented at an **International Conference** held in Vancouver. The proceedings begin with a broad, non-technical examination by the two editors, **Herbert G. Grubel**, Professor of Economics, Simon Fraser University and **Michael A. Walker**, Director of the Fraser Institute, of the relationship between "moral hazard", unemployment insurance and the rate of unemployment.

In Parts One and Two, the participating economists examine, empirically and theoretically, contemporary experience of national programs for dealing with unemployment in nine countries: in the **United States (Daniel S Hamermesh);** **Canada (Ronald G. Bodkin** and **André Cournoyer); New Zealand (Geoff P. Braae); Sweden (Ingemar Stähl); Belgium (M. Gerard, Herbert Glejser** and **J. Vuchelen); Ireland (Brendan M. Walsh); France (Emil-Maria Claassen** and **Georges Lane); Federal Republic of Germany (H. Konig** and **Wolfgang Franz); and Italy (Paolo Onofri** and **Anna Stagni).**

In Part Three , to add an historical perspective, two papers examine British social insurance systems — the 19th century Poor Laws **(Stephen T. Easton)** and the unemployment relief of the 1918-1939 inter-war period **(Daniel K. Benjamin** and **Levis A. Kochin)**.

400 pages	21 charts	18 pages of extensive bibliographical references and notes
82 tables		$14.95 paperback ISBN 0-88975-008-4

Out of Print Fraser Institute Books:
Available on Microfilm from Micromedia Limited, 144 Front Street West, Toronto, Ontario M5J 2L7.

PROVINCIAL GOVERNMENT BANKS: A CASE STUDY OF REGIONAL RESPONSE TO NATIONAL INSTITUTIONS by J. Benson (136 pages: 12 tables) ISBN 0-88975-020-3.

THE REAL COST OF THE B.C. MILK BOARD: A CASE STUDY IN CANADIAN AGRICULTURAL POLICY by H. Grubel and R. Schwindt (78 pages: 6 charts: 6 appendices) ISBN 0-88975-013-0.

Housing & Land Economics Series

RENT CONTROL: MYTHS AND REALITIES
International Evidence of the Effects
of Rent Control in Six Countries

Drawing on experiences in six countries over the last 50 years, a group of economists, including Nobel Prize Winners **Friedrich Hayek** and **Milton Friedman**, discusses the myth and the reality of rent control. The authors present definitive evidence that, in the final analysis, "there is no case for control."

Other contributors to this Fraser Institute critique of rent rent control include **George Stigler** (University of Chicago), **Bertrand de Jouvenel** (SEDEIS, Bureau of Economic Research, Paris), **F. W. Paish** (University of London), **F. G. Pennance** (late of the University of Aberdeen), **Sven Rydenfelt** (University of Lund, Sweden), **Michael A. Walker** (Fraser Institute), **Frank Kristof** (Rent Stabilization Association of New York City), **Basil A. Kalymon** (University of Toronto), **Ted Dienstfrey** (California Housing Council), **Richard Ault** (Louisiana State University), and Editors **Walter Block** (Fraser Institute) and **Edgar O. Olsen** (University of Virginia).

A surprising feature of this book is that a group of economists of a variety of ideological persuasions comes to a unanimous conclusion about the effects of rent control.

256 pages $7.95 paperback   ISBN 0-88975-033-5

ZONING:
Its Costs and Relevance for the 1980s

This provocative book raises a number of questions about zoning, specifically about recent variants of land-use controls. It forthrightly challenges underlying assumptions and principles at the root of the zoning philosophy and is required reading for all those concerned with the future of cities.

Authors are **Michael A. Goldberg**, Visiting Scholar (1979/80), Harvard University and Professor, Urban Land Economics Division, Faculty of Commerce and Business Administration, University of British Columbia, and **Peter J. Horwood**, a Vancouver Planning Consultant; with **Roscoe H. Jones**, Director of City Planning, Houston, Texas (the only North American city with no zoning regulations) and **David E. Baxter**, a British Columbia Urban Land Economist. Editor is **Walter Block**, Senior Economist, the Fraser Institute.

168 pages   3 maps   6 photos $4.95 paperback   ISBN 0-88975-032-7

PUBLIC PROPERTY?
The Habitat Debate Continued

ssays on the price, ownership and government of land. dited by **Lawrence B. Smith**, Associate Chairman, Depart- ent of Political Economy, University of Toronto and **Michael Walker**, Director of the Fraser Institute.

welve Canadian economists examine the operation and mportance of land markets and the impact of government egulation, control and ownership on the supply and price f land. Essential reading for all those concerned with the uture of landownership in Canada.

ontributors include: **David Nowlan** of the University of oronto (on the land market and how it works); **Larry R. G. Martin** of the University of Waterloo (on the impact of gov- rnment policies on the supply and price of land for urban evelopment); **Stanley W. Hamilton** and **David E. Baxter**, oth of the University of British Columbia (on government ownership and the price f land); **Jack Carr** and **Lawrence Smith**, both of the University of Toronto (on public and banking and the price of land); **James R. Markusen** and **David T. Scheffman**, oth of the University of Western Ontario (on ownership concentration in the urban and market); **Stuart McFadyen** of the University of Alberta and **Robert Hobart** of he Ministry of State for Urban Affairs (on the foreign ownership of Canadian land) nd **Michael A Goldberg** of the University of British Columbia (on housing and land rices in Canada and the U.S.).

278 pages   7 charts   20 tables $9.95 hardcover   ISBN 0-88975-017-3

ANATOMY OF A CRISIS
Canadian Housing Policy in the Seventies

n this book **Lawrence B. Smith**, Associate Chairman of the Department of Political Economy at the University of Toronto, and one of Canada's leading urban economists, considers the content and objectives of Federal housing policies from 1935 to the present. His conclusions that 1) housing policy is more and more being used as a vehicle for redistributing income in Canada and 2) that this policy is at the same time destroying the private sector's incentive and ability to supply housing, make the book required read- ing for everybody concerned with housing in Canada today. The book contains a comprehensive bibliography.

55 pages   7 tables $3.95 paperback   ISBN 0-88975-009-2

THE DO'S AND DON'TS OF HOUSING POLICY
The Case of British Columbia

Economist **Raymond Heung's** book is a case study of housing in British Columbia. As well as taking vigorous issue with the methodology and conclusions of the Jaffary and Runge reports, (issued as a result of a B.C. government-funded Interdepartmental Study), Heung's book provides a useful and detailed framework for housing market analysis, together with an examination of the costs of adopting a housing allowance scheme for British Columbia. This scheme, guaranteeing access to basic accommodation for all residents in the province, would cost less than half as much as current government outlays on housing in the province. The book, written by a former staff member of the government study team, has a message applicable to every province. As such, it should be of interest to everyone concerned with Canadian housing economics.

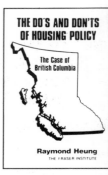

THE DO'S AND DON'TS OF HOUSING POLICY

The Case of British Columbia

Raymond Heung
THE FRASER INSTITUTE

145 pages 4 charts 28 tables $8.00 paperback ISBN 0-88975-006-8

PROFITS IN THE REAL ESTATE INDUSTRY

A controversial question never far from the headlines is the subject of profits in the real estate industry. In this book, **Basil Kalymon** of the University of Toronto's Faculty of Management Studies concludes that profits in real estate do not significantly deviate from those earned in investments in other industries. Kalymon examines the question in a scholarly and highly readable manner and vigorously enters the debate on equity compensation and the comparative performance of publicly-owned real estate companies and developers vis-à-vis other sectors of Canadian industry.

PROFITS IN THE REAL ESTATE INDUSTRY

Basil A. Kalymon
FACULTY OF MANAGEMENT STUDIES
UNIVERSITY OF TORONTO
THE FRASER INSTITUTE

59 pages 8 tables $2.95 paperback ISBN 0-88975-016-5

 TIMELY AND THOUGHT PROVOKING BOOKS PUBLISHED BY THE FRASER INSTITUTE AVAILABLE AT YOUR LOCAL BOOKSTORE, OR BY MAIL FROM THE INSTITUTE.

BOOK ORDER FORM

To: The Fraser Institute,
626 Bute Street,
Vancouver, British Columbia,
Canada. V6E 3M1

Please send me:

_____ copies of _____

_____ copies of _____

_____ copies of _____

Please add $1.00 for postage and handling

Enclosed is my payment in full of $ _____ or charge to:

Visa # _____

Mastercharge # _____

Expiry Date: _____

Signature: _____

Please send me information about membership in the
Fraser Institute . . . . □

please print

Name: _____

Title: _____

Organization: _____

Address: _____

_____

_____

please include postal code